DEAR CAREGIVER

Reflections for Family Caregivers

BY

Sharon Vander Waal

xulon PRESS

"Never will I leave you,
never will I forsake you."
Hebrews 13:5b

Sharon Vander Waal

Introduction:

My Care-giving Story

I was a caregiver for four and a half years to my husband, who had a devastating neurological disease. Sadly, my husband died on January 2, 2011. Having been a caregiver myself, I know that care-giving is a stressful and sometimes discouraging venture. It is my desire that my experiences during those four and a half years will not be wasted. It is my passion to perhaps identify with and help other family caregivers.

In 2006, my husband Wayne and I had already weathered the challenges of raising a family, including a few times of unemployment. The most recent time of unemployment had been in 2003 when Wayne's company (for whom he had worked for 39 years) moved out of country. In April of 2006, Wayne had been employed for over two years. In many ways, we were enjoying our "empty nest" time of life.

Then, in April of 2006, Wayne went in to see our family doctor for a routine check-up. It so happened that an intern doctor saw Wayne before our regular doctor came into the room. This intern noticed that my husband's speech and gait were not quite right. The upshot of all this was that an MRI was ordered for Wayne. The MRI showed deterioration or shrinking of his cerebellum. Wayne was then referred to a local neurologist and ultimately to Mayo Clinic in Rochester, MN. We were at Mayo Clinic for over a week in late August of 2006, and we also returned to Mayo Clinic in October of that same year for a few days.

Mayo Clinic believed Wayne had a rare neurological disease called Multiple Systems Atrophy Type C. It has some Parkinson disease-type characteristics, but it moves faster. The prognosis is eventual total disability. Wayne's disease affected his speech, balance, small motor skills, and a host of other involuntary body activities. Although he still ate well, later in the disease Wayne had to have his liquids thickened. This was to prevent those liquids from slipping down too quickly and going into his wind pipe.

In the midst of this came my own diagnosis with breast cancer in July of 2007 and my subsequent eight months of treatment to fight my cancer. I praise the Lord that, as far as I know, I am now cancer free. My care-giving role was, in many ways, a more difficult role than was the cancer victim role. The emotions that surface with such care-giving can be intense at times. I missed and mourned the way things used to be in my relationship with Wayne. Also the physical demands (like pushing wheelchairs and helping him with the lift) were very heavy. Finally, more of the decisions fell on me.

After being diagnosed with his disease in 2006, Wayne still worked for some time. Between the summer of 2006 (when Wayne was diagnosed with his disease) until January 2 of 2011 (the day of his death), Wayne went from still working, to walking with a cane, to a walker, to a wheelchair, and then the need for us to get him to a standing position with a sit-to-stand lift in order to transfer him from place to place.

We were told from the beginning that life expectancy is 6-10 years after diagnosis. Wayne lived only four and a half years after diagnosis, however. On January 2, when my son and I went to wake Wayne up for the morning, we discovered that he had died sometime during the night. We were not expecting his imminent death, and hence it came as a total shock.

Since I grieved each step down that Wayne took during his illness, however, I had anticipated that with his eventual death I would have an easier time with the grieving process. I did not find that to be the case. I grieved what Wayne had to go through, and I grieved what I went through. I grieved Wayne's absence. I have learned, however, that pain has a purpose, and pain does not equal peace. I had to make many baby steps towards healing.

These challenges of the last few years have drawn me closer to my Lord God and strengthened my faith and character. If it was not for the promises and encouragement of God's Word, however, I would have folded under pressure long ago.

· ·

· ·

Care-giving and God's Word

There are so many negative emotions which can accompany care-giving. These emotions often are intense. In many situations, care-giving involves seeing the one that you love deteriorate step by step before your very eyes. As a caregiver for my husband battling with a serious neurological disease, I too experienced many of these emotions. On December 23, 2008, I wrote the following comments:

> Lord, help me in my struggle to remain humble, patient, kind, and unselfish in my dealings with my husband. Help me concentrate on the blessings I (we) still have and not on the way things used to be. Help me to not be angry, but joyful.

Fill me with Your wisdom and lack of fear about the future. Sometimes it is tempting to feel all alone in this, Lord. I know that isn't true. Many people care, but they do not fully understand. Why do the prayers and concern always seem to be about the one sick and not the caregiver? Yet I know many people are praying, Lord. Most of all, I know You understand, Lord. Thank you that You are in control. I wish I could cry more, Lord; but You understand when my heart is weary and sad. I praise You for the hope I have in You, Lord.

Fear, discouragement, impatience, grief, and feelings of being overwhelmed are all emotions which can accompany care-giving. One of the things I learned through my years of care-giving is that I could not do it myself. I had to lean heavily on God's promises in His Word, the Bible. I needed to dig deeply into God's Word. I needed to do whatever it took to get God's Word into my heart and into my mind. God had an answer for every negative emotion and challenging care-giving situation that I faced as my husband's caregiver. I still need to remember that as I mourn his death.

Care-giving is so busy and time consuming. Take time in God's Word each day, however, dear caregiver. It is so important to your well being, both emotionally and spiritually.

God in the Loneliness of Care-giving

*A*s a caregiver, I sometimes felt intense loneliness. Usually, my husband Wayne (for whom I was caring) was right there with me in the room; and yet I felt a deep sense of loneliness. Of course, these feelings of loneliness greatly deepened after my husband's death, but they were also there while he was still alive.

I think these feelings of loneliness came from my grief over my husband's steady decline. Because of this decline, I could not and did not relate with him in the same way as I had in the past. I missed the way our relationship had been. So there was loneliness for that past relationship. There was a longing for the ability to communicate and talk things through as we had before.

There was a hunger for the fun times and for more of that spiritual and emotional connection we had experienced together. There was sadness in seeing him sleep away so much of his days and life being consumed with just meeting basic needs.

There was also a feeling of discouragement in knowing that others could not really understand and identify fully with all that Wayne and I were experiencing. It was a feeling of being all alone in this experience.

I found that reaching out to fellow caregivers online was a great help. Writing down my own feelings in this way helped to crystallize those feelings. It also helped me to connect with other caregiver bloggers, and it made me realize that I was not alone in my care-giving experience.

Most importantly, however, was my reliance on God, prayer, and His Word. God's promises to me in the Bible were a great comfort and help. He promised me and continues to promise me in Hebrews 13:5b that He will never leave me or forsake me. He also promised and continues to promise me that He will bring good in my character and life through the difficulties.

Dear caregiver: When you feel lonely, trust that God is with you even when no one else seems to understand. His love and care for you are awesome and marvelous.

The Caregiver's Caregiver

*A*s a caregiver for my husband before his death, it seemed as if my energies and concerns were mostly all directed towards his needs. In such a scenario, it was easy to long for some tender loving care directed at me and my needs. In January of 2009, I posted the following comments on an online blog site:

I am feeling some better after my stomach flu—a little tired yet. When I go to the doctor for post cancer treatment check-ups, it would be nice to have my husband with me. When I broke my foot, it would have been nice not to have had to drive in to the doctor's by myself. It would have been nice to have received a little TLC from my husband when I was in the midst of the worst of my flu symptoms. I praise You Lord, however, that You are my great Caregiver, Shepherd, and Savior. Thank You that I am beginning to feel better after the flu. Thank You for Your daily blessings. Please help me to remain dependent on You.

My husband, because of his disability, could not provide me with the care-giving that I myself needed, but my great heavenly Caregiver and Shepherd could do exactly that. In Isaiah 40:11 God says that He is my Shepherd who gathers me — His lamb — into His arms and carries me close to His precious heart. That verse was a beautiful reminder of God's loving care for me as a caregiver. God Himself is the Christian caregiver's Caregiver! Isn't that an awesome thought, dear caregiver?

Your Noblest Hour

During the years that I was a caregiver for my husband, it was easy to feel discouraged and impatient at times. Care-giving for someone who is continually declining in his health is a difficult and challenging experience. People would sometimes say that they admired me for taking care of my husband as I did. Sometimes people said things like, "You are so strong," or "You are a good example of perseverance in your Christian life." I felt somewhat guilty when they would say that. I am, and was, not strong at all.

Were it not for God's grace and strength, I would have really fallen apart during those care-giving years. I hadn't chosen or wanted this role in life at all, but it was the path God had assigned me. I just wanted for us to be a "normal" couple. Daily, I had to ask God for grace and strength for this role. Even at that, it was a constant struggle to fight against the negative emotions. I was constantly aware that I was a very imperfect vessel that God was using in caring for my husband.

Dear caregiver, I am sure that you have experienced similar emotions at times. Be aware, however, that your care-giving days are important and significant days in your life. You are an imperfect human being, but you are doing a very important work in God's kingdom. Also, you are doing for your care recipient what no one else would do. You have stepped up to the plate and you are doing the job of caring for your loved one even though, perhaps, no one else has chosen to help you in this endeavor. This, dear caregiver, is your finest and noblest hour.

The Caregiver's Grief

*C*are-giving for someone you love can be demanding and exhausting. If the person for whom you are caring has an illness without a cure and continues to decline before your very eyes, care-giving can become very discouraging. It can then feel like a grief process that is inescapable. The trouble with this kind of grief process is that one never comes to complete resolution, because when one has accepted one step backwards in one's loved one's life, another step backwards appears on the horizon.

As a caregiver for my husband for four and one half years, I experienced many of these emotions. I was a part of a wonderful online support group. This was very helpful, and I would recommend it to anyone who is a family caregiver. There were also many people who were praying for my husband and me, and much kindness was shown to us. It is amazing at times like this to find out who really shows care and concern, and who does not. Sometimes the care and concern is shown from those from whom we least expect it, and it is not given by those whom we would expect to show love and concern.

In spite of all this, I often felt alone in this process. It was I, after all, who basically dealt with the vast majority of the grief and challenges of helping my husband meet his daily needs as he declined step by step. I did have the Lord God with me, however. I know He was with me step by step, guiding me even when I was at my lowest points emotionally.

I also know He identified with me. The shortest verse of the Bible says, "Jesus wept," (John 11:35). Jesus further felt crushed with grief when His friends were sleeping and not praying with Him and for Him in His greatest hour of trial just before He was put on the cross (Matthew 26). As well as being my Savior, He understood and identified with my every weakness, sorrow, and need as a caregiver to my husband (Hebrews

4:15-16). Other people are not fully able to understand and identify with the caregiver's heartache. The Lord God can identify, however. Dear caregiver, trust that the Lord God truly understands your grief, discouragement, and worries. He truly identifies with you, and He truly can help and comfort.

Divine Purpose

$\mathcal{I}$ am the kind of person who likes to organize and plan for events in my life. I like to know where I am going and plan for all possible scenarios. I also don't like a lot of changes. While caring for my husband during his illness, I was not allowed that luxury. There were continual changes in my husband's health, and most of these changes were downward.

These downward changes in my husband's condition were very discouraging to me. How I longed for things to be "normal" in our household. From the beginning, however, I sensed that there was divine purpose in all we were experiencing. I sensed that I had spiritual lessons to learn through the care-giving experience.

For one thing, my experiences as a caregiver for my husband revealed to me things that were not right about me yet. They revealed my tendency to be impatient and to worry about the future. The difficulties of care-giving tended to draw me closer to God, and it thus made me more aware of these imperfections and sins in my character. This more profound awareness of these things in my life and God revealing these things to me were actually methods God was using to show His love to me as His child. God was trying to develop more Godly character in me.

My care-giving experiences were difficult and heart-breaking, but they were not without purpose. Besides helping me realize things that needed refining and correcting in my character, they made me draw closer to God. They also made me realize that I needed to rely on Him entirely if I wanted to be strong to do the things that I needed to do as my husband's caregiver. Self-reliance and thinking I could do it myself had to go out the window. There had to be a total surrender to God. I certainly did not come close to doing all this perfectly, but I definitely was made aware of these things.

There was also purpose for my husband, as his body declined in its ability to function as it should. I am not able to speak for him as to the exact spiritual lessons he learned. However, my husband taught me one important thing through his example. He never said, "Why me?" throughout his entire experience. That in itself was part of his purpose, trapped as he was in his body, especially the last months and years of his life.

Dear caregiver, believe there is purpose for the difficulties you are experiencing as a caregiver. Search for these purposes and lessons. Also believe with all your heart that your loved one, for whom you are providing care, has a wonderful purpose for being on this earth.

Hope

I wrote the following words in April of 2011, a few months after my husband's death:

The last couple days have been beautiful in my town. It has finally begun to feel like spring. Even though it has been a cold spring this year and spring has been long in coming, spring reminds me of new life and hope. The appearance of robins several weeks back was an indication that spring was on its way. The promise of spring reminds me that, just as winter is finally fleeing, so the heartaches of life are not forever.

Care-giving for a loved one with a prolonged disease can be very discouraging. Witnessing the gradual but ever increasing deterioration of a loved one's health is extremely disheartening. It can feel like the winter of life with no end in sight and no sign of hope for the future.

As a caregiver for my husband with a serious neurological disease, I often felt discouraged. As his mobility and a host of other issues continued to decline, I sometimes felt overwhelmed and stressed. This became especially true when transfers became more and more difficult. As a Christian care-giver and child of God, however, I knew that there was always hope. I knew that my hope was an eternal hope. As I was going through the care-giving journey, hope and my relationship with my Lord were what kept me going and persevering.

So what is hope? While I was a caregiver I wrote the following words about hope:

Hope reminds me that I do not really have to be in a state of panic. Things will work out in the end, and I will be guided step by step. Hope tells me that care-giving will never be easy, but there is an eternal purpose to this all. God's purpose will be fulfilled in me, and His love is with me. Hope tells me that what I do in care-giving is important, and it has eternal consequences. Hope tells me that the trials of care-giving are forming my character to become stronger. It reminds me to not focus on what I see, but on what will be and on what is good in my life right now. Hope focuses on seeing the small miracles of each day and knowing and trusting they will continue.

Hope is a great ally to have in facing care-giving challenges and in facing the challenges of life in general. Hope helps to promote wellness and joy and peace in the midst of the challenges. Dear caregiver, do not give up hope. Embrace hope in the same way as you embrace the hope and newness of spring.

Affirmations of Love

$\mathcal{B}$eing a caregiver for my husband for over four and a half years was a significant calling that the Lord God placed on my life. Its purposes in both my life and in my husband's life were far reaching, and the experience taught valuable spiritual lessons.

Those days were also laden with challenges, however. My husband's continual decline downward in his health robbed us of so much. It robbed us of the relationship we had experienced together in the past. Later in my husband's disease, I missed the easy verbal exchanges we had had in the past. Also in the past my husband had always been so free with expressions of his love. I would often long for those days. I wrote the following comments on May 17, 2009:

Before my husband's illness, he would tell me I was beautiful and he would often call me "his favorite wife." It became a standing source of teasing between us, because my reply would always be, "How many wives do you have?" My husband was always good about giving loving cards on special occasions also. So much of that verbal affirmation is gone now. My husband's speech is so poor that basic communication between us is difficult. I miss also the basic bouncing of ideas between us.

I knew that my husband still loved me, in spite of him not expressing it in the same way as he had in the past. More importantly, I knew God loved me with an eternal love. I knew that God also affirmed that love over and over again in the Bible. One of my favorite verses in the Bible is Zephaniah 3:17. In that verse, God told me and continues to tell me that He loves me and even delights in me! He actually rejoices over me, and He quiets me with His love. Furthermore He, the mighty God, will always be with me.

Knowing that God loved me and even delighted in me was a source of comfort to me during my care-giving days. God's affirming love for me comforted me even more than knowing that my care-giving role had a purpose and meaning.

Dear caregiver, if you are God's child, trust that the Lord loves you with an awesome and eternal love. When the discouragement and negative feelings surface, may you rest in God's love and find your treasure in Him!

Purpose Now
and for the Future

*C*are-giving is a purpose-filled calling. It may not be recognized as such by the world at large, however. Caregivers will not usually earn medals or receive honors for what they do day in and day out. Care-giving work does not facilitate the earning of great amounts of money, either. In fact, just the opposite is most often true. Care-giving for a family member can be discouraging and involves sacrificial giving of oneself to the person who needs one's help. It is, however, one of the most significant and purpose-filled callings God can give us.

Care-giving often involves a lot of heartache and grief, as we see our loved ones continue to move backwards in their health. In spite of this, the caregiver is engaging in God's work. Not only is care-giving filled with purpose while the caregiver is in the midst of the responsibilities of care-giving, but this phase of the caregiver's life is also a preparation for what God has planned for his or her post care-giving days. It has been said that God cannot use someone in a significant way until that person has suffered some deep loss, hurt, or pain. The losses and grief caregivers experience as they see their loved one's health deteriorate will help them to be more compassionate servants of God in future days.

Dear Christian caregiver, the challenges of care-giving are shaping your character to become a more beautiful reflection of Jesus. Think of the Bible characters like Job, Paul, and others. Through their losses and grief they became more dependent on the Lord and more useable in His kingdom. Because of your sacrifices in care-giving and because of the pain you feel while caring for a loved one who cannot recover, you are being prepared to also be used in significant ways when your care-giving days end.

You Need to
Take Care of Yourself

" *Y*ou need to take care of yourself." How many times have caregivers heard this? As a caregiver, one may be tempted to think, "I am so busy attending to the needs of my loved one. How can I possibly find time for myself?" However, as a caregiver for my husband with an ever deteriorating neurological disease, I found that it was essential to at least seek to take care of myself. This was not selfish. It was important for me to take care of myself so that I would not fold under the pressure and become ill myself. It was also necessary for my husband's well-being. I could be the best I could be in meeting my husband's needs only if I was also taking care of myself.

A caregiver needs to attend to his or her emotional needs. If there is a face to face caregiver support group in one's community, that might be helpful. If a caregiver knows someone else who is a caregiver, that also might be beneficial. By forming a relationship with that person, a caregiver may have found someone in whom he or she can confide. As a family caregiver, I personally found a lot of emotional support through an internet online support group and through blogging. Through reading other caregiver's blogs, I was greatly helped and reassured that my feelings were normal and often very similar to other caregivers. Through blogging my own thoughts, I was also able to crystallize my feelings. This helped me so much. Also, a caregiver needs to get out and do enjoyable things alone or with friends from time to time. If this means asking someone to come in and tend to the caregiver's loved one's needs, then that is what has to happen. Total isolation is never good for anyone's emotional needs.

A caregiver also needs to attend to his or her physical needs. A caregiver has to protect his or her own needs in order to be able to attend to the needs of the loved one who requires their constant care. One way one can do that is through a healthy diet and exercise, whenever possible. Exercise is a great stress reliever, and it can help to prevent a lot of diseases.

Further, a caregiver needs to attend to his or her spiritual needs. It is so important to develop an intimate spiritual relationship with the Lord. It is also important to stay deep in His Word, the Bible, and to constantly pray for the Lord's guidance and strength. Without my relationship with the Lord and the wonderful promises in His Word, I think I would not have been able to hold up under the stresses of care-giving.

Finally, a caregiver must be willing to ask for help. A caregiver must ask for help from God, but also some-times from others. As a caregiver, I did not want to ask for help. Also, sometimes I did not know what kind of help others could give me. In the end, however, I realized that I absolutely could not do it alone. I had a C.N.A. lady come in two to three nights a week at bedtime, and at the very end my son was able to greatly step up and help also. In this way, I was able to keep my husband out of the nursing home. In other cases, a nursing home may be the only and best option. A caregiver must have the courage and humility to accept and even pursue help as needed. Take care of yourself in every way you can, dear caregiver!

Identity

*O*ur identities are so often wrapped up with our various roles in life. Our identities, however, really should be a reflection of who we are inside. Our identities should reflect our values, passions, likes and dislikes, and our tastes.

My husband, Wayne, and I were married for over 39 years. During that time I was his wife, lover, and best friend. I was also the mother to our three sons and later a mother-in-law and a grandma.

During the last years of my husband's life, I also took on the role of my husband's caregiver. As my husband's caregiver I was often bombarded with questions like, "How is Wayne?" I never knew how to answer that question. Outside of a miracle, my husband was NOT going to get better; only worse. He was not going to get over his disease like the common cold. There was no treatment for his disease, and his symptoms were predicted to continue to deteriorate. So how was I to answer a question like, "How is Wayne?" People knew this, and I still was asked that question. I also felt that I was more than my husband's caregiver, and I didn't constantly want to be identified only as Wayne's caregiver.

As my husband's wife and caregiver, I grieved each step backwards that he took in his disease. It was painful seeing the love of my love deteriorate before my eyes. The role of being his caregiver did become almost all consuming. Because of this, it also almost became my identity. After my husband's death on January 2, 2011, my new status became "widow." I now had/have to work my way through the grief process and struggle to find a new purpose and role in life.

As we said before, however, our identities are not equal to our roles in life. Our identities should reflect our inner beings and passions. The roles we play in life should merely be a vehicle for fleshing out our identities. Also, as Christians, our true identities are really only found in our relationship with our Lord. That relationship will get us through the most difficult of challenges and trials.

Dear caregiver, the care-giving role can be so consuming that you forget who you are as a person. In the midst of the overwhelming decisions and challenges of care-giving, it is important that you do not lose sight of who you are as a unique individual. Most importantly, do not lose sight, Christian caregiver, of your significant identity in Christ.

Why?

*A*s a caregiver, have you ever asked the question, "Why"? I am sure that I consciously or unconsciously asked myself at one time or another, "Why did my husband get this awful disease? Why are people older than him walking around seemingly healthy and carefree? Why does this disease have to rob us of the relationship we once enjoyed? Why was I assigned the often discouraging and always challenging task of care-giving?" Seeing my husband deteriorate before my eyes during those care-giving years was very discouraging to me.

These are not easy questions to answer. We can give general answers to these questions, but the whys of the specifics of our lives are sometimes mysteries. We do know that we live in a broken world. The world was created perfect, but sin entered the world through Adam. Through Christ, we as believers are forgiven and restored to a relationship with God. We do still temporarily live in a broken world, however.

We also know that God has a master plan, but we do not fully understand why He allows certain painful things in our lives. God never promised us a life free from heartache. To the contrary, He said that there would be trouble, heartache, and challenges in this life. He also said that He will give us peace in the midst of it all (John 16:33). God further uses the challenges to mold our characters to be more like Him.

Knowing these things does not answer all of our "why?" questions, however. Some of the answers to these questions will remain a mystery in this life. Some of these secret things that we do not understand need to be left with God (Deuteronomy 29:29). This is because God is so much above us that we do not have the capacity to understand Him. He just wants us to trust Him. These "why?" questions remind us that we, as human beings, are not ultimately in control. Sometimes caregivers have to fight so hard for the well-being of their loved ones that they may lose sight of the fact that they really are not in control of the situation. Everything ultimately belongs in the hands of God.

Perhaps a better question than the "why?" question would be the question, "What can I learn through this, and how can I grow through this care-giving experience?" Another question might be, "How can I bring glory to God through this whole care-giving experience?" Yet another question might be, "How can I put one foot in front of the other and continue to persevere?"

Dear caregiver, trust that God has the answers when you do not. He does not give us the answer to all of our questions. Instead, He wants to give us Himself. We also need to trust that He has revealed enough of Himself so we can live lives of purpose and obedience.

Just Cry

As I go back and read my written thoughts during my care-giving days, I discover that I almost never sat down and had a good cry. As I look back on my posts, I am able to find only one time when I wrote about crying, even though I often experienced some very deep and negative emotions during my care-giving days. These deep and negative emotions were especially present as my husband's disease progressed. I very seldom cried, however. I cried much more freely after my husband's death.

I think as a caregiver I thought I had to be strong all the time, and so I didn't want to let go of my emotions and cry. I think many caregivers feel the same way. Seldom crying and letting those emotions come out of me was probably not the best idea, however. Crying occasionally is a good release for one's emotions. It tends to cleanse the soul, so to speak.

It is also good to cry out to God. We need to be honest with God about our every emotion, even the negative ones. God knows our feelings anyway, without our telling Him. Many of the psalms in the Old Testament are psalms of lament and crying out to God. In fact, there are more psalms of lament than psalms of praise. As long as we are turning to God, drawing closer to Him and not turning away in bitterness, it is good to cry out to God.

Dear Christian caregiver, just let the emotions come. If you do not want to cry in front of your loved one who is ill, find a quiet and private place to do so. Also come to God in prayer, and cry out to Him. Cry if you feel the need. Just cry!

Reality

The word *reality* can seem like a harsh word. It often reflects the gap between what we would like life to be like and the actual circumstances. In March of 2009, almost two years before my husband's death, I wrote about what reality had come to mean in my husband's life and in my life as his caregiver.

I wrote the following:

The reality I daily face is seeing my husband continue to have to use his walker for almost every step he takes. Reality is my husband sleeping 9-10 hours a night and still dozing in his chair during the day. Reality is that my husband's speech is so poor that communication between us is very difficult. Reality is very seldom seeing a smile on my husband's face. Reality is that there will most likely come a day in the future when I will not be able to take care of him by myself. Reality is that life is not like it was for many years of our married life. Reality is seeing this disease slowly taking more and more from my husband's ability to function in this world. Reality is discouraging sometimes.

As I mentioned before, my above comments were written in March of 2009. Reality, in actuality, became even harsher. Before my husband's death in early 2011, his mobility and a host of other issues declined even more. By that time, my husband had graduated to a wheelchair and we needed a lift to transfer him from place to place.

Even in March of 2009, I knew that there was also another reality in place, however. In that same journal post, I wrote the following:

Reality, however, is also knowing that I am not in this alone. My Lord and God is with me every step of the way. He will give me the strength and courage to press on. My Lord God will continue to add many blessings in my life, also. Reality further is knowing that there are many people who care about us and are praying for us.

Care-giving was the task that God had given me to do. It was not the task or life for which I had aspired. The life of my dreams and which I had envisioned was much different than reality. I am sure the same is true for you also, dear caregiver. The gap between what we envision and reality as we live it forces us to run to God. Our Lord God is our great Reality. He is unchanging. He also loves us and promises to never leave us alone.

It is also God who places us where we are in life. Even in the challenges and grief of care-giving, care-givers are right where they belong. They are doing what God has called them to do. In the measure they accept and receive this set of circumstances humbly, quietly, and thankfully, they will be blessed; for they are indeed doing God's work!

The Wise Caregiver

Care-giving is one of the most challenging endeavors an individual may have to face in life. This is especially true if the loved one for whom one is caring is either terminal or enduring a long-term illness. In such cases, a grief process already begins to take place the day of diagnosis. I know it did for me. As a caregiver, if I had not had a solid faith foundation, I would have folded under the emotional and physical pressure of care-giving.

That reminds me of the parable of the wise and foolish man in the Bible (Matthew 7:24-29). The wise man built his house on the rock. When the rains and winds came and the streams rose, the wise man's house stood because it was built on a solid foundation. The foolish man built his house on sand. When the rains and winds came and the streams rose, the foolish man's house fell flat.

This parable is so applicable to care-giving with all its heartaches, storms, and challenges. Wise caregivers will dig deeply into God's Word. They will hear, read, and obey God's Word. They will rest in God's promise that He will always be with them and never forsake them. They will believe the Lord their God when He tells them of His love for them. They will look for and trust God's guidance and strength in facing the discouragement and sometimes agonizing decisions of care-giving.

Wise caregivers will often experience difficult emotions and even spiritual storms as they go through their care-giving experience. They sometimes feel as if they will not be able to hold up under the pressure of the whole care-giving experience for even one more day. When that happens, they once again look to God for strength to face each moment of every day. Wise caregivers have learned that they should not seek to be self-reliant, but they must rely entirely on the Lord God. They know that their lives are based on the sure promises and the sure foundation of the Bible and of Lord God Himself.

Dear caregiver, make sure you are not trying to persevere in the storms of care-giving alone. Perseverance is a good virtue, but sometimes we have to reach out to other people for help. We are not meant to live this life in the power of our own perceived resources. Most importantly, we have to make sure we are relying on the sure foundation of God's Word, the Bible, and on a saving faith in the Lord God. The storms of care-giving are often extremely intense. Hence, it is essential that we are standing on God's sure foundation instead of the unstable sands of our own feeble efforts.

The Lord Understands

$\mathcal{E}$ach of us has unique struggles as we walk through this life. Few of us are free from difficult challenges. Taking care of my husband while he continued to decline due to his neurological disease was one of those very difficult and challenging experiences that I faced. For over four and a half years, my husband continued to decline in his health, and he became increasingly dependent on me until his death on January 2, 2011. I wrote the following words while I was caring for my husband:

Lord, give me grace and strength for this role. Others do not really begin to understand what I am experiencing, but You do, Lord. Thank You for that, Lord.

The challenges of care-giving can be intense. As a caregiver, one can feel so alone. Only a fellow caregiver can begin to understand the intensity of the emotions that accompany caring for a loved one who has an incurable disease. As a caregiver, sometimes people would say things to me like, "You are so strong," or, "You are a good example of perseverance in your Christian life." This would often make me feel somewhat guilty when they would express such thoughts. I was not strong at all. Were it not for God's grace and strength, I could not have continued to persevere. I did not choose or want that role in life, but it was the path God had assigned to me. I just wanted to be a "normal" couple.

When people would say such things it not only made me feel guilty sometimes, but it also made me feel more alone in my struggles. It almost gave me the feeling that I had to live up to a certain image of strength. When people instead would say that they were praying for me, I was truly blessed. Those people who gave me physical help were also a gift from God to me.

The truth of the matter is that another human being is not able to possibly understand all our physical, emotional, and spiritual struggles. Only God can do that. On a later date, I wrote the following words:

> My Lord is always advocating for me, and He fully understands everything I am experiencing. Other people may not fully understand, but my Lord does. If I could only keep that truth in the forefront of my mind, always.

Dear Caregiver, others will not always understand and identify with the struggles you experience. Know and rest assured, however, that the Lord identifies with your every need. He also cares about you deeply. He will supply you with the guidance, grace, and strength you need to meet the challenges of each new day.

Look for the Blessings

As a caregiver, I often found myself over-whelmed and discouraged with the challenges of care-giving. It was so easy to focus on the negative aspects of care-giving and forget about the blessings which still overflowed in my life. The Lord wanted me to, first of all, focus on Him and not on the challenges. He also wanted me to recognize the many blessings which He daily gave me. On February 6, 2009, I wrote the following words:

It is so easy to feel sorry for myself when I think about what both my husband and I have gone through in these past few years, but I have so many blessings yet. I have a home, food, clothing, and the love of family and church people. Most of all, I have my Savior who loves me.

In the Biblical parable of the prodigal son, the older son became jealous and angry when the father lavished gifts on his returning, formerly wayward son. The father said to this older son, in effect, "Why are you jealous?" He went on to say, "You are always with me, and everything I have is yours." I also always have my God with me even in the hard times, and every spiritual blessing God has, He has given to me. Yes, life is very difficult sometimes; but this life is not all there is. Also, my God provides joys and blessings even in this life. If I could only keep focused on that beautiful truth, always.

As a caregiver, I needed to remember God's past workings in my life, and I needed to look for and be thankful for His present blessings and workings in my life as well. I definitely saw God working in my life during the care-giving years. During my care-giving days, my husband's mobility capabilities deteriorated to the point that, by late 2010, I knew I could not continue to take care of him by myself. At that low point in my life, my son was able to greatly step up and help. Soon after that, I heard about a sit-to-stand device which we could also use with my husband. I believe with all my heart that God was leading me step by step. Again I learned, however, that I had to look for the workings and blessings of God in my life. I also learned that an attitude of gratitude is essential. On Feb 7, 2009, I wrote the following words:

I wonder if difficult times in our lives sometimes make us more appreciative of the little joys and blessings. Thank you, Lord, for daily blessings, even the ones we do not always recognize.

Dear caregiver, when you become overwhelmed with the difficulties of care-giving, focus on the Lord. Also look for His workings and blessings in your life. It will keep you encouraged to persevere in the challenges of being a caregiver.

Storms

*L*ike the storms of nature, the storms of life can come in many forms. Sometimes we know a storm of life is brewing on the horizon. Sometimes it comes unexpectedly. Either way, we usually cannot choose our life's circumstances. We do have a choice, however, in our responses to life's storms.

I was not prepared for the "storm" of my husband's diagnosis with a devastating neurological disease in 2006, followed by my own diagnosis of breast cancer in 2007. I am thankful to report that today I am a survivor of breast cancer. The same was not true for my husband, Wayne, however. For over four years, I saw his continual decline until his death in January of 2011. In 2009, I wrote the following words:

Care-giving, like the weather, always has its ups and downs. Some days feel stormy, and on those days I feel I can't do it anymore. On other days, life tends to take on a certain rhythm and pattern and is workable. Life always tends to be a mixture of joys and sorrows. I am joyful in my faith and in my relationship with my Lord. I am thankful that I know He is always with me. It is difficult living with the reality of my husband's disease, however. I am happy that the struggles of life are making me stronger in my character, in my faith, and as a person. I struggle with the fact, however, that it sometimes has to be so emotionally exhausting, and I wonder why life has to be so difficult.

One of the things the storms of the heartache and pains of care-giving taught me was that I could not rely on my own strength and that I really was not in control of anything. I think this is an especially difficult lesson for a caregiver to learn. This is because caregivers are constantly fighting for the best health and well-being of their loved ones. This need to try to control and do it in our own strength has to be offered up to God on the altar of surrender, however, if we are going to be strong in the storms of life.

During my care-giving days, the Lord was also trying to teach me that concentrating on the pain and heartaches of the storms of life often can blind us to the rainbow of the Lord's presence in our lives. We have to look for the wonders and workings of God in our lives. We have to look for His presence. Out of the heartache and brokenness, He can make something beautiful in His perfect timing.

Dear Christian caregiver, the storms of care-giving — and life in general — can be very brutal, and even devastating. Know that the Lord has the answers when you don't. Know that He is with you each step of the way. Know that He is in control, and He is very present in your life and in the life of your loved one. Finally, know that He sees your stormy days and loves you through the storms of care-giving.

The Difficulties of Going Away

O ne of the difficulties I experienced as my husband's
caregiver was trying to transport my husband to
places outside of our home. On May 17, 2009, I wrote
the following:

> Yesterday, at my husband's suggestion, we went
> out to eat. He so seldom wants to go anywhere, let
> alone suggest it, so I readily agreed. It was very
> windy, however, and so we took the wheelchair.
> By the time I had wrestled the wheelchair in and
> out of the trunk of the car, gone through the buffet
> line for my husband and then for myself, and then
> basically carried on a conversation with myself
> during lunch, I began to wonder if it was worth it.

Sometimes my husband, Wayne, and I were invited to eat with some of my husband's family. That was enjoyable, as it gave my husband and me a chance to get out of the house. Yet going out to eat with my husband's siblings presented me again with the same struggles of helping my husband in and out of the car and into the restaurant. When I saw other couples both in good health, I was happy for them. It did make me long for those days when the same was true for us also, however. I longed for a "normal" life.

Most Thursday nights we would go to our local son's family's home for supper and the evening. My son was always so helpful in getting my husband in and out of the car and into their house. First, we did this with a walker. Later, we had to use a portable ramp and the wheel chair. My son was always helpful when he was with us, but so often I struggled alone when we left home to go places.

I always knew that there was a divine purpose for all that was happening in my husband's and my lives. I knew all things would work for my ultimate good as a child of God. I knew I still had overflowing blessings in my life, but that did not stop the sadness in my heart at seeing my husband's body deteriorate. It also did not stop the struggles of providing for my husband's needs.

I certainly did not choose the care-giving role that God had assigned to me those years during my husband's illness, but I do know that God was with me each step of the way. As difficult as it was, I would do it again. I had to cling very closely to the Lord during those days, as I still need to do now. The Lord God had to give me the grace and strength for this role. He was with me in my unique struggles. He guided me, loved me, and forgave my many moments of impatience. Dear Christian caregiver, the Lord God is with you also. He knows your unique struggles and heartaches. Lean into His strength. Trust His love for you.

God's Great Love Story
for You

*I*f I were to write a book about the story of my life, I wonder what events in my life I would include in my writing. Would I write about all the sad things that I have experienced in my life, or would I concentrate on the joys of my life? What about the care-giving chapter of my life? Would I concentrate on the discouragement and grief of seeing my husband continually decline in his health and eventually pass away, or would I concentrate on the blessings and joyful moments of my life even the midst of care-giving?

What about you, dear Christian caregiver? If you were to write an autobiography of your life, what would the story of your life be like? My guess is that you would share many special and joyful moments, but I am equally convinced you would share moments of heartache and pain. No matter whether you would be sharing joyful moments or sorrowful moments, however, as a child of God the chapters of your autobiography would reveal that your life's story is a love story. Your life's story is a story of God's love for you. In fact, perhaps especially in the difficult moments of your life's story, God's love for you would shine forth the brightest.

The pain and discouragements of some of life's circumstances do not define who we are. God's unfailing love for us in all circumstances shapes who we are now and who we are becoming by His grace. If no one else knows or loves us, God does. God's love for us is everlasting. It never fails (Jeremiah 31:3). God's love for us is passionate and comforting. It is also a powerful and personal love. God actually says that He delights in us! (Zephaniah 3:17.)

As we become more and more spiritually rooted in the knowledge and experience of God's love, we begin to grasp the vastness and depth of His love. His love for us is so great we will never fully understand it completely, but in the measure that we do begin to understand the fullness of His love, we will be filled with the fullness of God Himself in our lives. We will slowly begin to reflect Him more and more in our lives. Also, we will begin to see in deeper ways His workings, love, and guidance in our lives.

Your and my life's stories with both their difficult moments and pleasant moments are beautiful stories of God's love for us. We are also part of God's story for the world around us. Even when we do not understand the tragedies of our lives, God still loves us. We just have to trust and rest in His love for us. Dear caregiver, as you face the heartaches, difficult decisions, and challenges of care-giving; never forget God's love for you! Your experiences are part of God's great love story for you!

Shifting of Roles

"*It's* becoming difficult to remember what it felt like when he wrapped me in his arms, and I felt secure and wanted instead of motherly and needed." Such was a comment made by Jennifer, a woman on an online care-giving site. Those words so echo the feelings I experienced as a caregiver for my husband. My husband's neurological disease robbed him of so much. It also robbed our relationship of so much. When a relationship becomes a caregiver to care receiver relationship, things change.

For a period of time during the progression of his disease, my husband Wayne enjoyed listening to audio books. One day almost three years into the progression of his disease, Wayne was listening to an autobiography about a man who suffered through MS. My husband's disease was a different and (I would say) a worse neurological disease, but there was much in the book with which my husband could identify.

While my husband was listening to this audio book on this particular day, I overheard a few comments made by the author of the book. The man was speaking about how much the disease had robbed them of his and his wife's relationship with one another. He said that their relationship had become more of a mother or caregiver to a child relationship than a wife to a husband relationship. I also felt the loneliness of that reality so often myself with my husband's disease. That shifting of roles was so difficult sometimes. I loved my husband, but this was not how I had envisioned living our retirement years.

I look back now with pleasure on the many good years my husband and I had together. I thank God for the blessing of a husband who loved me, protected me, and was my life's companion. His disease and subsequent death changed that. Life has a way of changing things. So is there anything in life we can count on not to change?

My Lord God never changes. Although my husband could not be there for me as he had been in the past, God was there for me. When I longed — and still long — to be wrapped in my husband's arms, my Lord wraps His arms around me. He is my source of security and joy.

Dear Christian caregiver, sometimes the pain of caregiving can be so intense that it is difficult to feel God's presence, peace, and joy. His presence is with us at all times, however, in spite of our feelings. Trust Him. Rest in Him. In the measure you do this, you will begin to feel His presence above the noise of your pain. You will feel His arms wrapped around you in love. You will feel His strength.

Care-giving and Forgiveness

*F*orgiveness and struggling to forgive is always a part of any grief process or sense of loss in one's life. Furthermore, there is a grief process that accompanies long term family care-giving. I know as I witnessed my husband's health continue to decline step by step, I definitely went through a grief process.

Whom, then, might we need to forgive in the grief process that often accompanies care-giving? First of all, we need to accept God's forgiveness of ourselves. As a caregiver, although devoted to my husband and my marriage vows, I was less than perfect. I often felt impatient. I know there were times that I said and did things which showed this impatience and which were not up to God's standard of love.

To reject God's forgiveness for these things would be a slap in the face of God. God pardons and forgives our sins. In fact, He delights to show us His mercy; and He smashes our sins underfoot and throws those sins into the depths of the sea (Micah 7:18-19). I also tended to put false guilt on myself at times for things that were out of my control. These too needed to be turned over to the Lord. I suspect this is true of most every caregiver at one time or another.

Secondly, we need to forgive others. Unless others are caregivers themselves, they cannot begin to understand the heartaches and challenges of being a caregiver. Hence, they may say trite and hurtful things. Also, the people who one may think would be most likely to step up and help are often not there to assist. Either they are not able to empathize because they have not gone through the same care-giving experiences, or they have issues and responsibilities of their own. They also may not feel emotionally equipped to get into the process of helping. As a caregiver, however, one has to let go and forgive. We are commanded to forgive, and a lack of forgiveness will only add to the emotional struggles which sometimes accompany care-giving.

Thirdly, it is also necessary at times for a caregiver to forgive the loved one for whom one is caring. No human being is perfect, and the caregiver's loved one will not always show the love and gratitude to the caregiver that he or she might expect. As a caregiver, I remember thinking that it would be nice to be thanked occasionally for all that I did for my husband. I do know my husband loved me, however, and we have to forgive and overlook these things. We need to forgive these things because Christ has forgiven us. We also need to overlook them for our own emotional health.

Finally, we need to be careful that we do not blame God for our loved one's ill health and for the trials of care-giving. We will never understand all the "whys," but our best course of action is to trust our Lord God and to run to our Lord for strength and comfort.

Back to Reality

Seeing my husband gradually lose all his mobility and ability to care for himself due to his neurological disease was a very painful experience. However, during the course of my husband's illness we did have a few opportunities for some memorable and enjoyable times. In spite of his lethargy at home, my husband also seemed to enjoy these times.

In August of 2009, we met my siblings and my mom at a motel in La Crosse, WI. My siblings and mom came from Minnesota. We were coming from the other end of Wisconsin, so it was a half-way meeting place for us. Thursday through Sunday of that week, we enjoyed fellowship together and sightseeing opportunities.

On Saturday, we all went on a Mississippi River cruise. That was beautiful, and the boat that we went on for the cruise was wheelchair accessible. We even saw bald eagles on our cruise on the mighty Mississippi. That weekend, they also surprised me with red roses and a birthday cake in celebration of my birthday. In spite of having to deal with Wayne's disability during that trip, it was a fun time of interacting and laughing with my siblings. It proved to be a huge blessing to my husband and me.

This experience proved to be a wonderful reprieve; but when we returned home, reality set in again with full force. There were so many issues with Wayne's disease that made life a constant struggle. There were also blessings, however. The challenge was to concentrate on those blessings.

Dear caregiver, treasure the wonderful moments in the midst of the heartache and chaos of care-giving. Even after those treasured moments pass and you go back to the reality of the day to day of care-giving, continue to look for the blessings. The realities of care-giving can be so harsh. There is another reality, however, dear Christian caregiver. That reality is the reality of God's love for you.

Nevertheless

I happen to enjoy reading novels with an Amish setting and Amish characters. I also enjoy reading Christian historical novels. I think I like these kind of novels because they portray a simpler way of life. In spite of this, however, the characters often have similar struggles and emotions; as we all do as human beings.

Some time back I completed a novel trilogy in which the main character, Hannah, undergoes a number of very difficult trials and struggles. In spite of all these difficulties, she struggles through the bitterness and hurt, and she comes to the realization through her faith that there always is a "nevertheless" in every overwhelming and sad circumstance in her life. I thought that was such a wonderful concept that I made a picture with the word "nevertheless" on it. I then framed it and put it on my kitchen counter.

As my husband's caregiver, there were many emotional struggles as I saw my husband's health deteriorate step by step before my eyes. Also, about a year after my husband was diagnosed with his disease, I went through eight months of treatment for breast cancer. *Nevertheless*, I grew in character during this time. Sometimes during those difficult care-giving days and after my husband's death on January 2, 2011, I have felt all alone. *Nevertheless*, the Lord has been with me through it all, and His presence in my life has become increasingly real to me in a new way. During the years I was a caregiver for my husband, the Lord supplied love and help to me through others and through His presence, and He continues to do so today after my husband's passing to Glory.

"Nevertheless" is such a powerful word. It is such a liberating word. Dear Christian caregiver, there is always a "nevertheless" phrase that can be added to every heartache and challenge you face as a caregiver, and in life in general. Based on your own care-giving experience,

I challenge you to complete the following sentence for yourself, dear caregiver: Care-giving is often so discouraging and heartbreaking, *nevertheless...*"

God's Sure Love

*I*t is so difficult in our human minds to reconcile two truths. One truth is that God loves us. The other truth is that God allows us to face very difficult challenges and even suffering in this life. Sometimes, the challenges and suffering we face tempt us to doubt God's love for us.

Care-giving, by definition, is challenging at best. If a caregiver is put into the position of witnessing his or her loved one's health continue to deteriorate step by step, that caregiver might also experience discouragement, grief, and a host of other negative emotions. Though God's ways are difficult to understand sometimes, one truth to which Christian caregivers can cling is the truth of God's overflowing and certain love for them.

God is the very definition of love. We tend to think that when life is easy and comfortable, God must love us. Conversely, if things are difficult and challenging in our lives, we may be tempted to think God no longer cares for us. If we begin to see things from God's perspective, however, we realize that suffering and challenges have purpose and meaning.

Christian caregivers know that the emotional, spiritual, and physical challenges of care-giving are molding their characters. They know that (somehow) God is going to bring good out of the chaos, heartache, and overwhelming challenges of care-giving. They know that God will be with them each step of the way, supporting them and sustaining them with His love and power.

Dear Christian caregiver, rest in the truth of God's love for you in the midst of all the negative emotions that care-giving can produce. Trust that He, in His love, will lead you through this difficult process. Trust that good will come out of all of the heartaches and challenges of care-giving. Just rest and trust in His love.

Peace

Care-giving not only involves the tasks of caring for one's loved one, but there is also much emotional turmoil which can accompany the family care-giving process. I found this especially true in the later months of my husband's illness. Transfers to the bathroom, bed, and car were becoming increasingly difficult; and I was finding myself fearfully anticipating each transfer.

God wants us to do everything in dependence on Him. Care-giving began to teach me that self-sufficiency would not work. Apart from God, we can do nothing of eternal value. God's deepest desire for you, dear Christian caregiver, is that you depend on Him in every situation. There is no other way to travel through the challenges — and sometimes grief — of care-giving. Rely on the

Lord constantly. Let Him fill you moment by moment with His strength. You do not have enough strength on your own, dear caregiver, but He will give you enough strength for the day.

As I think back on my days as caregiver for my husband, I remember them as very difficult days. My husband's disease was a terrible one which made him completely dependent on others, especially near the end of his life. However, as I look back, I can see how God provided step by step through it all. I clung tightly to God during those days. Perhaps my emotional stress would have been lighter, however, if I had not tried to anticipate the future. I needed to rely moment by moment on God alone.

The Lord wants to give you His peace in the midst of the chaos of care-giving, dear Christian caregiver. Take time each morning to sit quietly in His presence through prayer and Bible reading. Then walk through the day constantly reminding yourself of His presence. The peace which will come from remembering His presence in your life is a rare and beautiful treasure. That peace will help you stand up under the struggles of the day. Wear God's peace throughout the day.

He will refresh you when you are weary, dear caregiver. He will give you what you need when you feel as if you cannot persevere for even one more moment in your care-giving duties. Also, do not become discouraged when your emotions so overwhelm you that you do not feel that peace, dear Christian caregiver. God understands our weakness. On those days, just turn once again to the Lord.

The Losses of Care-giving

*I*f your loved one has suffered with a terminal disease or with a disease which has caused a severe disability, your loved one has experienced serious losses in his or her life. You, as his or her caregiver, have also suffered serious losses. You have most likely suffered the loss of a relationship as it once existed and the loss of time doing fun things together with your loved one. Dear Christian caregiver, those losses can really hurt. I think the loss or change in a relationship that one once had with one's love one is the most difficult of all losses. You have also suffered a loss of dreams for the future. As a caregiver, you may have further lost the help of your ill loved one with duties around the house. Finally, because of the expenses of care-giving, you may have lost possessions and financial security.

In September of 2009 I wrote about yet another loss. This loss was the loss of my husband's leadership in decision-making due to his illness. I wrote the following words:

I do weary of being responsible for so many decisions. When we bought a different vehicle this summer, I did all the talking and dealing. When there are telephone calls to be made or problems to be solved, it is I who has to take charge. Soon, we will have some major insurance issues to consider. That will be mainly my responsibility. We may have a chance to move from our apartment to a condo. There is a condo in our price range available, but all the things to think about in regards to such a possibility are a bit overwhelming.

I love the good times my husband and I still have together, but I miss the way things used to be. I miss the times when my husband took more responsibility for these types of things and decisions. I miss the person my husband used to be.

The losses and the stresses of care-giving can be overwhelming at times. Always remember that the Lord God is with you in the losses, dear Christian caregiver. His plans for your future are also good. He can turn the chaos and heartaches of care-giving into something beautiful in your character and in your future. Rest in Him.

Panic or Trust

What do you do, dear Christian caregiver, when your care-giving responsibilities become increasingly overwhelming and you do not know what to do next? A few months before my husband's death, it was becoming increasingly difficult for me to take care of his physical needs. As a caregiver, maybe you can identify with some of the feelings that I experienced at that time. I hope my sharing those feelings will be helpful to you, dear caregiver. On September 25, 2010 I wrote the following paragraphs:

Things definitely are changing with my husband, Wayne. Transfers for my husband to the bathroom, back to the chair, etc. are getting more difficult and I have been finding myself becoming increasingly stressed. I find myself dreading and consumed with thinking about the next transfer. I also keep wondering what my next step needs to be. Keep doing it myself? Try to hire more in-home help? Pursue nursing home options?

Last night, my son came over. He was very stressed because of a serious job issue. He was basically in panic mode. It was and is a serious situation, as his job may be on the line. My first reaction was to think, "I do not need this. I have enough stress of my own."

Then, however, I found I could relate to him and thus calm him down. I told him about my heavy stress level and how we just need to trust. Nothing happens by chance, and we are being guided. I also told him that what will be will be, and we will be okay. I asked him if he had prayed about it, and he said, "Yes."

He then asked me to pray for him. I did that, and we both felt better. I do not think I could have helped him as much if I had not been as stressed as he was. I could relate to him, and therefore what I said to him had validity. It helped both of us.

This whole incident reminded me that everything has a purpose, even the difficulties of care-giving. Because of the stress I was experiencing with care-giving, I could help my son. We also shared a prayer and a hug together. That was a special blessing in spite of the situation we are both in. What could be more beautiful than that?

Dear Christian caregiver you do not need to live in a state of panic. The Lord will guide you step by step. Care-giving will never be easy, but God's purpose will be fulfilled in you through your care-giving role. What you do in care-giving is important, and it has eternal consequences. The trials of care-giving are forming your character to become stronger. Do not focus on what you see, but rather on what will be and on what is good in your life right now. Focus on seeing the small miracles of each day, and know and trust that they will continue. God's love is always with you, dear caregiver.

The Sunshine and the Rain of Your Life

Care-giving, like the weather, always had its ups and downs for me. As a caregiver, some days felt stormy, and on those days I felt that I couldn't persevere in my care-giving responsibilities any longer. On other days, life tended to take on a certain rhythm and pattern and was workable. In 2009, in the midst of my care-giving days, I wrote the following:

It is a rather cold, dreary day outside as I write my blog post. We have been having some rainy days of late, also. I guess we all prefer the warm sunny days, but we need the rain also. What a picture of our lives. The plants would shrivel up and die if they received only sunshine and no rain. So we would also shrivel up into something undesirable if we did not have the rain and the storms in our lives.

Care-giving, with its responsibilities, at times brings on a storm of emotions and/or dreariness of spirit in my life. Sometimes I long for the way things used to be before my husband was diagnosed with his neurological disease. Then, however, there would have been lessons in character-building and faith-building in my life that would have gone untaught.

Life always tends to be a mixture of joys and sorrows, but I think the experiences of care-giving tend to highlight these swings back and forth in one's emotions. As a caregiver, I was joyful in my faith and in my relationship with my Lord. I was thankful that I knew He was always with me. It was difficult living with the reality of my husband's disease, however. I was happy that the struggles of life were making me stronger in my character, in my faith, and as a person. I struggled with the fact, however, that care-giving often had to be so emotionally exhausting, and I wondered why life had to be so difficult.

I mourned the fact that my husband's balance issues, mobility, speech, and a host of other issues continued to decline. I mourned the flatness and changes in his personality from what I had known for so many years previously. However, I found joy in the times we spent with our grandchildren and in our pleasant times with family. I found joy in my faith and in the comfort and strength my Lord gave me. I found joy in the promises of God's Word. I found joy in the beauties of creation all around me.

The care-giving years were very difficult years in my life. I realized that I had to cling tightly to my faith in order to survive. I also learned that I had to look for the blessings in my life. Finally, I discovered that the joyful things in my life were definitely better because of the sorrows.

Dear caregiver, life is a mixture of joys and sorrows. There are a number of deep heartaches in caring for a loved one with a terminal illness. In spite of all this, look for the joys and blessings in the midst of the storms in your life. It will help you persevere.

The Caregiver's "I AM"

*I*n the Bible, God has many names. The names of God reveal His character. When God revealed Himself in the burning bush to Moses in the Old Testament, God said His name was, "I AM." God as the great "I AM" means that God is everything any human heart might need. God is even everything the caregiver's heart might desire and need.

Care-giving is often one of the most difficult challenges any individual might face in this life. Our God says He is with us in life's trials and difficulties, however. He says that He is the great "I AM." So how is God the great "I AM" in the caregiver's life? God says, "I AM the caregiver's strength. I AM his or her source of guidance and wisdom in the many decisions that need to constantly be made in regards to his or her loved one's health. I AM the Christian caregiver's peace in all the chaos and discouragement of care-giving. I AM patient and forgiving, and I AM love personified. I AM the caregiver's life, and I AM all he or she will ever need. I AM the caregiver's salvation and righteousness. I AM the caregiver's all in all."

When God calls people to the task of care-giving, He is calling them to a very important and significant task in this world. The challenges of family care-giving can be overwhelming and often are not pleasant, but nonetheless care-giving is a holy calling from God Himself. Likewise, when God spoke to the Old Testament Moses in the burning bush, He called Moses to another overwhelming, but God ordained task. You can read about it in Exodus 3 in the Bible. Moses did not want to undertake the task God had assigned him. Moses was afraid and filled with confusion. He felt overwhelmed by what God was asking of Him, and he felt that he was not able to do what God had asked of him. God reminded Moses that He would be with him each step of the way. He reminded Moses that He was the great "I AM." God would be for Moses everything Moses needed Him to be, so Moses would be able to complete the task that God had assigned him.

Especially during the last months of my husband's life, my care-giving responsibilities became very overwhelming. My husband could do next to nothing on his own, and the deterioration of his body was heartbreaking. I sometimes felt as if I could not continue in God's ordained task of caring for my husband for one more day. I am so glad I had the great "I AM" with me during those days and months and years.

Dear Christian caregiver, the Lord God is also your great "I AM." He is your all and all. He will be with you each step of the way, dear Christian caregiver, rest in faith in your great "I AM."

The God of Healing

As a caregiver, have you ever wondered why God does not heal your loved one's devastating disease? Why did your loved one get his or her awful disease in the first place? Jesus Christ performed many miracles during His lifetime. Why doesn't He perform a miracle in your loved one's life? As a caregiver, have you ever asked yourself these questions?

Jesus' miracles in the Bible prove that He is a God of compassion and a God of healing. It proves that He cares about people with great needs. These miracles also prove that He is the Son of God. They further prove that He is a promise-keeping God.

So why does God heal some people and not others? About a year after my husband was diagnosed with His serious neurological disease, I was diagnosed with breast cancer. After eight months of treatment — including chemo, a mastectomy, and radiation — I am still doing well several years later. After four and one half years of suffering the declines and indignities of his disease, however, my husband died on January 2, 2011. So, why was I healed and my husband was not?

God *is* a God of healing, and He *does* care about us, but He sees the big picture when we do not. He says to us as His children, "I am the One who was promised to you long ago. I am the One who saved you from your sins and made you My child. That in itself proves I am a God of miracles, and I have done a miracle in your life. I am the ultimate answer to all of your needs."

Some people believe that Jesus Christ's miracles prove that He will heal all of our bodily diseases. However, God sometimes has a reason for not healing all of our bodily diseases. Sometimes He has a greater purpose for those people who are not healed from their diseases. Often people can bring greater glory to God through their steadfastness in the midst of their disease.

For those who believe God will heal every bodily disease, God says, "You have missed the point of my healing! You just don't get it! You are so focused on what you hope to receive from Me that You have missed *Me*. I am the great God of the universe who loves you with an infinite love, and I want to give you much more than physical healing. I want to give you *Myself*!"

Dear Christian caregiver, embrace the God of ultimate healing and the God who will meet all your ultimate needs. Ask Him to give you a willing heart to embrace His plan and purpose for your life, even in the heartaches of care-giving and often seeing your loved one decline in his or her health. Embrace Him.

Letting Go

O ften, caring for a terminally ill loved one can become so overwhelming that it can stir up all kinds of negative emotions. I think this is also true of any difficult or heartbreaking life challenge.

I was a caregiver for my husband for about four and a half years. By the fall of 2010, my husband's disease had progressed to the point that he was pretty much dependent on me for everything. At that time, I found myself becoming increasingly stressed. By God's grace, through the extra help of my son and the use of a lift, we were able to navigate through that period of time. Little did I know at that time that just a few months later — on January 2, 2011 — my husband would pass into eternal life.

In November of 2010, I was challenged to write about my thoughts on the idea of letting go. Below are the words that I scribed at that time:

I want to let go of fear for the future. My husband's health is declining, and there have been significant changes lately. It is easy to fear the future, but I want to let go of fear and I want to just trust. I want to let go of fear and replace it with trust, faith, and peace. I also want to let go of the daily stress or any form of self-pity that I feel, and just take a more peaceful attitude towards the events of the day. I want to approach them calmly, step by step.

I want to let go of "what ifs" from my thinking. I want to let go of how I wish things were in my life, and I want to truly accept things as they are. I want to let go of both the expectations I have in my life of myself, and the perceived expectations I think others have of me. I also want to let go of the expectations I have of others. I want to let go and watch God work.

Dear Christian caregiver, what negative emotions do you need to work on releasing? Releasing them will add to your peace, and even joy.

Out of the Mouths of Babes

On most Wednesday mornings, I give my daughter-in-law a little respite by helping with my granddaughters' home schooling. I did this for her even before my husband's death on January 2, 2011.

One day in the middle of November of 2009 when I was helping with home schooling, the girls sang a Scripture song they were learning for their Bible class. It was based on the Scripture passage in Jeremiah 29:11 which tells us that God has good plans for our lives and wants to give us hope and a future.

I asked my granddaughters that day, "Is this true even when sad things happen?"

They said, "Yes."

So I said, "What about Grandpa not being able to walk?"

They had to think about this, but still said, "Yes."

Then one of my granddaughters said, "One good thing is now that Grandpa can't work, he can come to the Thursday night suppers at our house." Out of the mouths of babes; finding little blessings in difficult situations.

Those words from my granddaughter's mouth that day in 2009 reminded me that I needed to strive to see the blessings in my life and to not focus on the difficulties and challenges of my care-giving role at that time.

Later that month on November 25, 2009, I wrote the following words:

A care-giving friend of mine said the following concerning family care-giving, 'I've never known anything so heartbreakingly difficult, but yet it can be so rewarding and feels like a gift." Our care-giving role is a difficult gift that has been given to us.

So often I feel that I could do without this difficult "gift" in my life. I often long for the days when things were different. If I am honest, however, I know I have grown spiritually, emotionally, and in character through this experience. If I am honest, I still see many other blessings in my life also.

Dear caregiver, there are many heartaches and challenges in being a caregiver. This is especially true if you are caring for a terminally ill person and only see declines in his or her health. In spite of all these things, dear Christian caregiver, keep your focus on the Lord and not the problems. Look for the blessings — it will add to your joy! May you find a thankful heart even in the difficult times, for in this way you will also find true joy. May God bless you richly for your role as a caregiver!

Control and the Caregiver

Caregivers, by their nature, tend to be planners and well-organized. They have taken on responsibility for the care of another human being who needs their help. They also often have to be advocates for their loved ones, and they often have to fight through the "red tape" of government rules and the medical profession. Hence, as a caregiver there is a tendency to feel that one always has to be in control. In the end, however, none of us are in ultimate control. Only God is in control. We are mere instruments in His hands.

As a caregiver, I too often felt as if I had to keep things under control. Deep in my heart I knew, however, that I needed to release these things to the Lord. Caregiving was too overwhelming to try to try to "keep all the balls in the air" under my own power. In the summer of 2009, while I was in the midst of my care-giving days for my husband, I wrote the following thoughts:

I am enjoying my Wed. night women's Bible studies so much. They apply so much to what I am going through in this whole care-giving scenario. One thing we talked about last Wed. night was that our attempts to grip so tightly to *our* plans and *our* control of things are pointless.

Our control of things is really an illusion. God is the One who is in control. So all we have to do is rest in God where He has placed us and experience the freedom of following Him. Where He has placed me in life as a caregiver is not always easy. I am trying to continually remind myself, however, that I could have less feelings of stress if I would always completely rest everything with God. I have so many things that need my attention in the next weeks, and it is difficult attending to these things on my own when I was accustomed to my husband taking care of many of these kinds of things. I am not alone, however; God will direct me as He has in the past. Now, to keep remembering that!

Dear Christian caregiver, care-giving is probably the most difficult job you have ever experienced. It can be physically, emotionally, and spiritually overwhelming at times. Trust that the Lord God is in control of it all. He will guide you. Remembering that will lighten the load.

Rejoice

I wrote the following words about a month before my husband's death:

At first glance, it would seem ridiculous to associate rejoicing with care-giving. The last years have been very difficult years for my husband and me, and yet when I look back there is so much for which to be thankful. There is so much for which I can rejoice.

In April of 2006, Wayne was diagnosed with his neurological disease. It is called Multiple Systems Atrophy type C. It is affecting his cerebellum. Between the summer of 2006 when Wayne was diagnosed with his disease until now

(December of 2010), Wayne has gone from still working, to walking with a cane, to a walker, and now to a wheelchair. Wayne's disease affects everything. It affects his mobility, his balance, his speech, his eating habits, and even his personality.

The emotional feelings that surface with care-giving can be intense at times. Every change downward is emotionally draining and scary. Also, the physical demands of care-giving are heavy. Finally, more of the decisions fall on me now. So, what is there to rejoice about in this situation? For one thing, I know that I am becoming a much stronger person through all this. I am having to do things I never did before. This is good, as it has strengthened by character and confidence.

More importantly, it has strengthened my faith and my love for my God. Over and over, I have seen things fall into place when I felt I could no longer hold up. Most recently, my husband could no longer help me with transfers, as he lost his ability to stand up on his own. I thought I would have to put him in a nursing home. Right when I was at my lowest point of despair, my prayers were answered by the ability of my son to step up and help. Also, I was able to procure a sit-to-stand lift. Even though the lift is a clumsy, heavy piece of equipment to use, it is an answer to prayer. I have seen over and over again this kind of answer to prayer. So, I am sad about my husband's illness; it is the heartbreak of my life. But I rejoice in the provisions from above.

I also rejoice in my three sons and their wives. I rejoice in my wonderful grandchildren. I rejoice in their beautiful and sweet spirits and in their love for their grandpa and me. I rejoice that I am a breast cancer survivor. I also rejoice in the sun, which is shining today after many cloudy days. I rejoice in the daily blessings. Lord, help me to remember these blessings when I become sad or overwhelmed with the challenges of care-giving.

Dear Christian caregiver, the challenges and heartaches of care-giving are always present, but the blessings are there also. How can you rejoice in this day?

Gifts

We often associate gifts with special occasions like birthdays and Christmas, but there are gifts that we are able to receive any time of year. As with every gift, however, we have to open our hands to receive it; otherwise, the gift does not benefit us or give us any joy. The best gifts we can receive, however, are the gifts God desires for us!

The Lord offers us the gift of salvation. He further offers us the accompanying gifts of joy, peace, and hope. They are ours for the taking; and yes, dear Christian caregiver, they can coexist with the pain and heartache which often are present in family care-giving. Further, the Lord promises us a happy ending. That happy ending is eternal life. Christian caregiver, the heartaches that sometimes accompany care-giving are but a comma in your life story. They are not the end. They are not the end of your loved one's life story, either.

Further, we are able to receive the gift of trust in God. We receive this gift by resting in Him and by letting go of anything we are holding on to too tightly or trying to control. As a former caregiver, I know how much we want to stop the progress of our love one's disease, but much of this is beyond our control.

Forgiving others who have not been there for us is a great gift we can give ourselves, as well as them. We are further able to receive the gift of forgiveness for ourselves. We must give the Lord any true wrongs and ask for His forgiveness. We often carry around a lot of false guilt about things beyond our control, however. So whether false guilt or true guilt, we need to let it go and give it to the Lord. Dear caregiver, receive the gift of releasing it to the Lord.

One great gift we can give ourselves is the gift of acceptance of our situation. We often waste so much energy wishing circumstances were different, but we can rest assured that we are right where we are supposed to be in our lives. Dear Christian caregiver, your responsibilities are emotionally overwhelming at times; but in the measure that you are able to accept where God has placed you now in your life, you will find joy. It is a great gift to give yourself. Yet another wonderful gift we can give ourselves is the gift of being still in the presence of God (Psalm 46:10). Doing this helps us grow in peace, wisdom, and insights. Finally, we can give ourselves the gift of gratitude. When we are grateful in spite of our circumstances, our joy and blessings will multiply and resentments will flee.

Christian caregiver, you have many challenges and sometimes you experience much emotional upheaval as a caregiver for your loved one. Would not these be wonderful gifts to have in your life?

Remembering

At times, the heartaches of care-giving can cause caregivers to temporarily forget the memories of the good times that they have experienced with their loved ones before they became ill. Caregivers can become so consumed with the challenges of fighting the declines in health evident in their loved ones that the good relationships and past good memories of their interactions with their loved ones get pushed to the back of their minds.

At one point during my husband's illness, I retrieved from their storage space our old love letters that we had sent to each other while dating. I spent an enjoyable period of time that day rereading those letters. It was so refreshing and a real spirit lifter. It helped to give me some perspective on things that day.

After my husband's death, I reminisced about special memories of our lives together. I recalled some special trips we had taken. I thought about how I enjoyed hiking trails with him from time to time before he became ill. I remembered our excitement over the birth of our children and grandchildren. I also thought about what I had loved and admired about him.

Dear Christian caregiver, perhaps your loved one's illness prevents you from doing some of the things you at one time loved doing together. Perhaps the illness has changed your loved one's personality and quality of interactions with you. Perhaps, however, remembering those good times and thinking about what you always loved and admired about your loved one would help you to get through the very challenging days of care-giving.

God is Sufficient

$C$are-giving for a loved one is often challenging, at best. Care-giving can also be heartbreaking and overwhelming if one cares for a loved one who continues to take steps backwards in his or her health. As a caregiver for my husband with a devastating and fast-moving neurological disease, I certainly found that to be true. In January, 2010, I wrote the following words about my husband:

> How far we have come from him being our family's primary breadwinner, my best friend, my lover, and my husband. He is still my husband, but how different our roles are now. How could our lives have gone from "normal" to wheelchairs,

incontinence products, and immobility in just a few years?

I resolved at the beginning of this year to look for the blessings and to also look for the faithfulness of my God in my life. I resolved not to stress so much. I am making a conscious effort to do this. I do see the blessings and faithfulness of my God. In spite of it not being a great day, I recognize blessings in my day even today. I really do, but these sad feelings are still there for what is no longer there.

Dear Christian caregiver, I am certain you experience many emotions of sadness and heartbreak also; especially if you are caring for someone with a long term illness. So where can one run for help with these negative emotions?

The only source of strength and guidance in the challenges of life is the Lord God. We must spend time in His Word, the Bible, and we must spend time in prayer. This will begin to instill in us an understanding of the depth of God's love for us. This, in turn, will provide us a peace that only the awareness of the presence of God in our lives can provide.

As we begin to look for the wonders of God (which are all around us), we begin to realize that we are not abandoned or left alone in this world. Dear Christian caregiver, your feelings may tell you that you are all alone. Daily remind yourself of God's truth, however. Seek His companionship and counsel. He alone can guide you perfectly as you navigate the often stormy waters of care-giving. God alone can comfort you completely as you struggle with the negative emotions which often accompany your care-giving days. The Lord God is sufficient, however. He is also greatly honored, dear Christian caregiver, when you set your affection on Him in the midst of the heartbreak of care-giving.

No Pit So Deep

*A*s a caregiver, you may sometimes feel as if you are in a deep pit from which you cannot escape. The emotions of being responsible for the well-being of your loved one who continues to decline before your very eyes can be overwhelming. Below are some words that I scribed on January 23, 2010. Perhaps you can relate:

Last night we watched the DVD *The Hiding Place*. It is about a Christian family in Holland who hid Jews in their home during the Nazi occupation in World War II. They were eventually found out and captured. The father died about 10 days after their capture, but the two sisters, Betsy and Corrie Ten Boom, were sent to a concentration camp.

In the horrors of concentration camp, Betsy and Corrie came to the conclusion that there was no pit so deep that God does not go deeper. That movie was a real encouragement to me. Sometimes care-giving can seem like a real pit, but the Lord is with me each step of the way. My life is a piece of cake compared to what those ladies endured.

Having said that, however, the fact remains that care-giving is often very difficult. I really have to struggle with patience and wisdom. Besides the difficult physical and mobility symptoms in my husband, I am seeing some slowing down in his thinking. It is not that I can't still rationally discuss some things with him but, as I said, there is a slowing down in thinking. He sometimes does have trouble controlling his emotions in public. This usually manifests itself in laughing. Then there is the always difficult task of communicating. He speaks with a mumble and does not speak clearly. Finally, I suspect some depression is going on also. This whole process of decline — physically and otherwise — that I see in my husband sometimes seems like a slow death.

Adding to this stress, we are planning on moving in about 4 weeks. We are scheduled to close on February first on our new condo. Then we are scheduled to have a wheelchair ramp built starting on February second. The plan is to move into our new condo on February 20. My prayer is that the ramp will indeed be built the week after closing and that it will be easily usable with my husband, Wayne. Sometimes my stress level feels like about twelve on a scale of ten.

Dear Christian caregiver, the stress of care-giving can often be overwhelming. It can feel as if one is in an emotional pit so deep that one is not able to crawl out of it. In those times, remember the conclusions of Corrie and Betsy Ten Boom: that there is no pit so deep that God does not go deeper.

A Thankful Heart

A thankful heart is something God expects of us. Thankfulness can also add joy to our lives in spite of adverse circumstances. Being a caregiver of a terminally ill loved one is one of life's greatest challenges and heartaches. Finding joy in the midst of it can seem like an impossibility. As a caregiver for my husband for four and a half years, however, I knew I needed to find things for which to be thankful in order to endure and survive emotionally.

It is best to start thanking God for His presence and peace. Then try to write down at least three things each day for which you are thankful. I did this while I was a caregiver, and I found it very helpful. No matter how difficult your care-giving situation, there is something for which you can thank and praise the Lord each day.

A thankful heart opens up the very windows of heaven. Thankfulness gives one a foretaste of heaven itself. In the process, these experiences provide even more reasons for gratitude because of the joy which enters one's life through the avenue of a thankful heart.

Thankfulness comes from focusing one's heart on the Lord throughout the day. It also comes from looking for His wonders and treasures. Remember, however, that sometimes these treasures come through pleasant experiences; and sometimes these treasures come through the difficult moments (see Isaiah 45:3). Valuable lessons are often learned in the dark and difficult experiences. Often, these experiences are the only way to learn dependence on God and trust in Him. This was and is certainly my experience as a caregiver for my husband and then during the grieving after his death.

At times it may feel so contrived to express thanks to God when we are feeling really down in the pits. Even then, it is best to express thanks, however. This is because thankfulness is the road to the presence of God and His peace. It is amazing, but in the measure we give thanks regardless of our feelings, God gives joy in spite of our circumstances.

Care-giving is often an overwhelming challenge. The difficulties and heartaches will not go away by simply pursuing a thankful heart. Those who are thankful, however, will be blessed even though their care-giving heartaches remain. Joy and pain can coexist. So, dear Christian caregiver, for which blessing will you thank God today?

A Subject We Like to Avoid

*D*ear Christian caregiver, there is a discussion we like to avoid. It is a topic, however, that would be wise to discuss with the loved one for whom you are caring. It would be especially wise to discuss this topic with your loved one if she or he is terminally ill. That topic is death.

My husband was diagnosed with a rare neurological disease called Multiple Systems Atrophy Type C in 2006. At the time of his diagnosis, a time frame of 6-10 years until death was thrown out. Any internet site I visited suggested the same time frame. In actuality, my husband only lived four and a half years after diagnosis.

A few times during his illness, my husband would say that he did not think he had long to live. At the time

I thought that those statements were merely depression speaking. This was logical in my mind, because depression can accompany neurological disease. I felt as if I did not want to feed into that depression. I would often say, "You don't know that. You could outlive me."

Now I believe that was a wrong approach on my part. I believe I should have openly discussed with my husband his feelings about death. It most likely would have been helpful to him on an emotional level to have talked about this with me. It also could have been the source of some deep spiritual discussions, as my husband was a believer and a child of God. Further, it would have helped me to better know his wishes for the funeral and other matters. I think my husband may have been more in tune with reality at that time than I. Perhaps I was in denial about how close to death he must be in view of his constant physical declines.

Dear Christian Caregiver, death is never a pleasant subject to discuss; but its reality is not going to go away by not discussing it. Consider discussing these matters with your loved one, especially if he or she brings up the subject. Your loved one's eventual death is not going to be hastened by your discussion of death with him or her. The date of that death is in God's hands.

Unless dementia prevents it, I would strongly suggest having an honest and open discussion with the loved one for whom you are caring. Openly talk about his or her eventual death. Remind your loved one that the process of dying is not something anyone would choose, but we will all experience it unless Jesus returns first. Also remind him or her, however, that death for the Christian is merely a gateway to heaven and being with the Lord.

Joy and Sadness

$\mathcal{L}$ife is such a mixture of joy and sorrows. This was especially evident to me on February 24, 2009. On that day, my little grandson was born. That day was also the day that my mother-in-law had her cancer surgery. Furthermore, at that time I was right in the middle of my care-giving days with my husband, Wayne. It was a time of constant declines in his health. Below is what I wrote on that day:

Our new grandson was born this morning! He weighed 9 pounds, 9 ounces and is 21 1/2 inches. His name is William Wayne; William for his great-grandpa and Wayne for his grandpa (my husband.) I took care of William's sisters while my son and his wife were at the hospital. This is our first grandson after six granddaughters from our three sons.

On a sad note, my mother-in-law had her cancer surgery also today. They were able to get much of her large tumor, but there are many little tumors that they could not get. Chemo will follow later, which will hopefully suppress — but not cure — the cancer. Even with all this, they say she most likely has 18 months to two years of good life before it will come back.

So today is such a mixture of emotions — joy over our new grandson and sadness about my mother-in-law. Lord, thank you for my precious new grandson born today! Please be with my mother-in-law tonight and in the difficult days that lie ahead. Give her Your peace, Lord. Give me peace too, Lord, as I see my husband continue to deteriorate. Grant me patience also, and help me to concentrate on the many blessings and joys in my life and not on the difficulties.

My mother-in-law passed away on September 2, 2010 from her cancer, and my husband passed away on January 2, 2011 from his disease. My grandson, however, is a healthy and delightful child. Yes, life is a mixture of joy and sadness.

Dear Christian caregiver, care-giving challenges — and life in general — can sometimes be very overwhelming. Remember, however, that even in the sadness of care-giving there are many joys. Look for these blessings. Remember that life on this earth will always be a mixture of joys and sadness. Know, however, that God will be with you each step of the way.

Thankful for Difficult Gifts

My husband was diagnosed with his neurological disease in 2006. That summer, our son and his family purchased our home in the country, and my husband and I moved to an apartment. We did this because we knew my husband's disease would get progressively worse. Therefore, we knew it would not be possible for us to remain living in our country home of 27 years. We first lived in that apartment for three and a half years, but in late February of 2010 we moved to a condo. On March 6, 2010 I wrote the following words:

It is two weeks ago today that we moved into our new home. I really do love it. I love seeing the sun streaming into the living room windows in the early morning. I love the fact that my husband's wheelchair is not blocking traffic areas nearly as badly as it did when we lived in our apartment. I am glad that my husband seems to like our new home, also.

Even in our new home, however, care-giving issues continue to press heavily on my spirit at times. So much of care-giving is just plain gross, thankless, and just not a lot of fun. I must remind myself that this is my calling right now. I must remind myself that this is developing my character and stretching my faith. I must remind myself that even the difficult "gifts" of life (the troubles and trials) are good if I don't become bitter in the process and try to see God's hand in even these things. Thank you, Lord, for Your presence in my life, for my family, for my friends, for my new home, for beautiful sunshiny weather, and for a host of other blessings. Make me also thankful in the difficulties of care-giving.

Dear Christian caregiver, are you able to find the blessings in your life in spite of the difficulties and challenges of care-giving? It is so much easier to dwell on the negatives in our lives than to remember the positives. Furthermore, dear caregiver, can you see the blessings in even the very difficult tasks and heartaches of caregiving? Are you able to see God's hand in the difficult "gifts" of life, the troubles and trials? May God bless you and help you as you fulfill this difficult but crucial calling in your life!

The Goodness of God

The years that followed my husband's diagnosis of his neurological disease in 2006 were the most difficult and challenging years I have ever experienced. The heartbreak of witnessing his continual declines was extremely difficult. Those years were also extremely stressful years. Being responsible for the well-being of the man I had loved for many years, not knowing how long I would be able to care for him by myself, and feeling so alone in all this was very challenging.

I still find myself thinking about those care-giving days at times. If it were not for the fact that I knew the Lord was with me during those care-giving days and in the days since my husband's death, I would not have survived. Knowing this has also given me — and continues to give me — joy in the midst of life's pain.

Quite some time ago I did a Bible study lesson on the goodness of God. The lesson reminded me of the good reasons why we suffer. It reminded me that God is more interested in our inward characters and conforming us to the image of Christ than in our comfort. Conforming us to the image of Christ is one of the reasons for trials in our lives.

The lesson went on to say that sometimes the pain seems to outweigh the best of benefits. We may understand reasons and answers in our heads, but those reasons do not always reach where it hurts in the heart. The challenges of care-giving or other life trials can be so painful that it is difficult to see how the growth in our character compensates for the pain we are experiencing.

Perhaps there are no answers to the "why" questions in our lives that will completely satisfy us. God does not always give us reasons or answers. God does something better than giving us answers, however. He gives us Himself. Also, He explained Himself on the cross. His goodness displayed in His sacrifice of Himself on the cross is really the only proof we need of His love and goodness. Believing in the goodness of God does not mean that the heartaches will completely disappear. It does, however, help us move forward and persevere in life.

I find those thoughts comforting. If I did not believe in the goodness and presence of God, I am not sure where I would be today. Thank You, Lord, for that blessed reality! Thank you that You are there in the moments of heartache.

Dear Christian caregiver, please turn to the Lord for strength and help during your care-giving days. Please do not turn away from Him, because you do not always understand His ways. Trust in His goodness.

Reliance on God

Perhaps you have heard the popular saying, "God never gives us more than we can handle." When I was a family caregiver, however, I discovered that I often felt overwhelmed and felt that God had given me much more than I could handle. I experienced these feelings even more strongly with each new decline in my husband's disease, especially during the last months of my husband's life when I could no longer physically take care of him on my own.

The truth is God never promised not to give us more trials and difficulties than we can handle *on our own*. In fact, God often gives us many more struggles than we can handle. God does this so that our eyes will be open to how desperate we are for Him and for His help and provision.

Rather than striving to be more self-reliant, we need to seek to become more God-reliant. As a caregiver, I learned that I just did not have the resources in myself to handle the challenges and heartaches of care-giving on my own, so I absolutely had no choice but to rely on the Lord.

As a caregiver, I also learned that I had to have help from others. I learned that God sometimes used others to help me. They became His instruments in helping me and in His kingdom. I needed to begin to root out my desire to be in control. The truth was, I never was in control of anything. God was in control, and I needed to learn to rely and trust in Him.

Dear Christian caregiver, what change would it make in your outlook towards your care-giving challenges and struggles, if you saw them as valued lessons in learning dependence on God? When you are at the absolute end of you own spiritual, physical, and emotional resources you can then begin to more fully depend on God's resources. Check out II Corinthians 1:8-9. Total reliance on God is a good place to be!

Looking for the Wonders

*A*s a caregiver, it was difficult to see the constant decline in my husband's health. It was difficult seeing the changes in him physically, but it was also difficult to witness the changes in the person I had once known. In late 2008, I began journaling my feelings at a blog site online. In order to survive, I also realized I needed to begin to look for the wonders and blessings which were still around me. On March 24, 2009, I wrote the following words:

What will be my attitude today concerning my circumstances? It is raining and dreary out today. I enjoy the sunshine more. However, we need the rain for the plants and grass to grow. So rain is good, and it is a blessing. I have also grown spiritually and emotionally through the "rain" and "storms" of my fight against breast cancer last year and through my present care-giving experience with my husband. So that is good, and it is a blessing.

The last couple of days have been spent filling out paperwork and also spent on the phone asking questions about this paperwork. I hate filling out paperwork. Filling out paperwork for my husband's disability and making necessary phone calls has helped us financially in the past, however. So that is good, and it is a blessing. One of the things I needed to do to fill out this paperwork was to get some additional information from our three sons. That has resulted in good and productive conversations. That is good, and that is a blessing. One of these calls to one of our sons resulted in my husband and I being able to hear our little 8 month old granddaughter (who lives with her parents in London) giggling in the background. What a joy! That is good, and that is a blessing. We just received a phone call and invitation to have supper with family. That is pure joy. I see no negatives there.

Lord, help me not to get bogged down with the negatives of care-giving. Help me to consider it a privilege, and help me to look for the blessings. Help me to look for Your wonders in my life.

Dear Christian caregiver, care-giving is probably one of the most difficult experiences you will ever undertake. That is often the case with a calling as significant as care-giving. In the midst of the challenges, negative emotions, and disappointments, however, also look for the wonders, dear caregiver. There are wonders and blessings in even the most difficult of days. Looking for the wonders will allow the joy to remain in your life, even in the struggles and heartaches of care-giving.

Preparation for the Valley

Seeking to provide for my husband's needs during my care-giving days could get emotionally heavy at times, but I feel my past experiences helped to prepare me somewhat for the care-giving challenges. One of these experiences actually coincided with the beginning stages of my care-giving days. That experience was my fight against breast cancer.

In July of 2007, about a year after my husband was diagnosed with his disease, I noticed a swelling in my right breast and under my arm. I was able to book an appointment with my physician's assistant. She sent me for a mammogram and MRI the next day. A couple days later, I received the devastating news that I did indeed have breast cancer and that the cancer had invaded my lymph nodes. The tumor in my breast was very large, and my doctor told me later that my lymph nodes were all gummed together.

A few days later, I found myself at my oncologist's office, and after a full body scan at the hospital I began chemo by the end of July of 2007. All together, I had eight chemo treatments in three week cycles, mastectomy surgery with all my lymph nodes under my arm removed, and six and a half weeks of daily radiation. Side effects of chemo were fatigue, mild nausea, food tasting like cardboard, and loss of all of my hair. Radiation caused some burning, but it was manageable. All treatment was completed in April of 2008!

Cancer treatments would not be something that I would want to experience again, but at the same time it was a time of blessing as well as hardship. It is difficult to explain, but I became freer in my spirit and less concerned about other people's opinions as a result of this cancer experience. I experienced the love of other people, and most of all I experienced the love of my Lord and Savior in a new and fresh way. I learned dependence on the Lord God during those many months, and I grew in my faith. The Lord's strength and His love to me were demonstrated through others who helped me through those months.

I am still miles away from having it all together. Just perhaps, however, I will be able to face today and the days ahead with God's strength because of my cancer experience and my experiences with the heartaches of care-giving. The memory of those days will never go away. It has changed who I am forever, mostly for the good.

I know that there will always be problems in this life, but I am further certain that my Lord and Savior will always be with me throughout my life. I know He will give me the strength to handle anything I need to face in the future. Even in difficult times, God has promised to be with me and bless me and someday take me to live with Him eternally. Dear Christian caregiver, rest in Him.

The Caregiver
and God's Presence

*W*hen I was in the midst of caring for my husband, I found great comfort in getting up early in the morning before my husband awakened and spending time in reading the Bible and caregiver devotionals, and in prayer. This time in the morning helped to remind me that my Lord was with me and present in my life each step of the way. Even now, I find my morning devotional time so important to my emotional and spiritual well-being.

However, as I encountered the challenges of caring for my husband, sometimes it was easy to get bogged down emotionally. This was especially true near the end of his disease when my husband could no longer help with transfers. It was easy in such moments to forget that God had promised in His Word to always be with me. It was easy to forget about His presence right beside me.

There is a story in the Bible in Luke 24 about two men who were walking along a road. Jesus had just risen from the grave, but these men did not believe that the happy resurrection event had occurred. As they were walking, Jesus came along beside them and started talking with them. Later, they sat down to a meal and began to eat with this "stranger" that they had met on the road. The Lord was right with them, but they did not recognize Him or His presence. Only later did their spiritual eyes open, and they recognized Jesus.

The same is true for us. The Lord God is right there with us, and so often we do not recognize His presence. As a caregiver, the Lord was with me each step of the way. I can look back and see that with absolute certainty. Yet, in the moments of care-giving, there were times when it was difficult to see that.

Sometimes we are disappointed and feel overwhelmed when life does not go the way we hoped it would. I very much would have liked to spend many years in happy retirement with my husband. Instead, my husband was diagnosed with a terrible disease, and I was thrust into the difficult role as his caregiver. It is easy at times like these to forget the Lord God's presence is right with us all the time. Sometimes we are so sad that we do not feel His presence or see His presence with our spiritual eyes.

That does not negate the truth that the Lord is always with us. I believe the Lord is especially with the caregiver who turns to Him and relies on Him. Dear caregiver, don't miss the Lord's presence right beside you. Pray that God will open your spiritual eyes so you can see and feel His presence.

Waiting

One day a caregiver on a care-giving site online wrote about her frustrations with always feeling that she had to wait. She talked about waiting for a doctor's office to call her back and waiting for lab results concerning her loved one. She talked about waiting for the next step. She talked about waiting for her loved one to get sicker and her eventual death. She also talked about waiting for a cure for her loved one's illness and wanting to wait for something good to happen, but seeming to only think of the reality of her loved one's illness and not the miraculous. She further talked about waiting for appreciation for all the things she did in her care-giving role and waiting for life to be normal again when she knew it never would be.

She also talked about her life consisting of waiting for potentially life and death decisions, and the pressure of knowing that she holds somebody's life in her hands by the decisions that she makes. Finally, she talked about waiting on God to show her how to fulfill her purpose. Looking back on my care-giving days, I can so identify with many of her emotions. We all would like to get better at waiting because we do not feel that we do a very good job of it.

Recently, I read a devotional on waiting which I thought was so applicable. The devotional pointed out that productive waiting involves waiting on God and directing our attention to Him in anticipation of what He will do. It involves trusting Him with every fiber of our being. It involves staying conscious of Him as we go about our daily activities. It involves total dependence on Him, realizing we cannot do it on our own.

I so remember those stressful care-giving days when I was caring for my husband. I so remember the heart-ache of all the declines and the dread of how I was going to handle the future declines. The truth is that God was with me every step of the way. I see that in an even more focused way as I look back on those days.

I think all the struggles (and waiting is part of those struggles) makes us stronger people. It helps to shape our characters. But this kind of character building is so painful, isn't it? In the struggles of my personal life in the last few years, I have often thought, "I could do with a little less character building now, Lord." You may have thought the same thing, dear caregiver, but there is a purpose in all this. It will also shape your future life.

Dear Christian caregiver, as my recent devotional went on to say: God does give blessings to those who wait on Him in the measure that they wait on Him. He gives renewed strength, hope, and an awareness of His continual presence. I fell so far short of resting in Him during my care-giving years. I often let stress and anxiety come to the surface. Knowing He was in control, however, helped me through those days. Rest in Him, dear caregiver. Wait on Him.

He Will Equip You

*D*ear caregiver, have you ever said to yourself, "I cannot do this any longer! Why has God laid on me the task of care-giving? Who am I to be asked to do this job? I am not equipped to do this job." As a former caregiver for my husband with a terminal disease, I remember thinking these things from time to time during my care-giving days.

In an Old Testament book in the Bible, God assigned a man named Moses an important task. It was an important task, but it was also an overwhelmingly daunting task. It would be a huge undertaking for Moses. Hence, Moses was understandably afraid. (Read about it in Exodus chapter three in the Bible.)

Moses began to make excuses for not being able to do the job God had given him to do. The first question that Moses asked God when God gave him his new assignment was "Who am I, that I should do this job?"

But Moses was asking the Lord the wrong question. Moses should not have asked, "Who am I?" The right question should have been, "Who is God?" Moses should not have been focusing on his own inadequacies, but he should have been focusing on the power of the Lord to help him. Moses should have been focusing on the faithfulness of the great God who had been faithful to His people in the past and who had promised to be with them in the future. Even though Moses continued to make excuses, ultimately Moses obeyed God and God used him in mighty ways.

Care-giving has to be one of life's most challenging tasks. Know, however, dear caregiver, that God is a faithful and dependable God. Completely trust in Him to always be with you and strengthen you. God is not just a God of glory and power. He is a faithful God who completely gives Himself to you. As God was with Moses in the past in the frightening and overwhelming task He assigned him, He will continue to be with you also in the sometimes overwhelming challenges of care-giving.

God has assigned you the task of care-giving, dear Christian caregiver. Because He has assigned you this task, He will also equip you. He will give you His strength as long as you need it. Our strength has nothing to do with ourselves. Our strength is wholly dependent on the Lord and His faithfulness. We must learn the secret of bringing our burdens to the Lord and leaving them there. God promises that He will be with us wherever He asks us to go and in whatever He asks us to do. Trust Him and lean heavily on Him, dear caregiver.

The Folly of Trying to Control

*A*s a caregiver, I remember sometimes thinking about the future and worrying about the progression of my husband's terminal disease. I remember worrying about how I would take care of my husband after he became completely disabled. As it turned out, the last months of my husband's life did become especially difficult; but the Lord also provided for those circumstances.

During the course of my husband's disease, in addition to worrying, I felt very much that what I did or did not do would influence the speed with which the disease progressed. I think I subconsciously felt as if I had some control over my husband's disease.

God, however, wants us to trust Him enough to let life's events unfold without striving to control or predict them. He wants us to relax in His unfailing love. When we try to predict or control the future in any way, we are trying to be self-sufficient. God wants us to rely on Him alone.

Caregivers are loving and strong advocates for their loved ones. They often have to be. They also need to be responsible in providing any medical help possible for their loved ones. One thing caregivers must remember, however, is that in the end they cannot control the progression of their loved one's disease. Only God can control this. Caregivers anxiously wringing their hands trying to control the uncontrollable can result in a losing out on the time they do have with their loved ones.

The better alternative to worrying about the future and trying to control the future is to live in the present moment, depending fully on the Lord God. When I think back on my care-giving days, I remember this was so difficult to do. Worrying and trying to control, however, leaves us fearing our own inadequacy. I remember those feelings also, dear caregiver. Instead, in all of life's struggles we need to rejoice in God's abundant supply of strength which He gives us for each difficult situation as it arises.

Dear Christian caregiver, do not divide your life into things you think you can handle by yourself and things for which you need God's help. The truth is you need help for it all. Rely on Him for every care-giving situation. Doing so will help you face each care-giving day with confidence.

Pruning

*D*ue to the kindness of others, I have received cut flowers from time to time. When we receive cut flowers, we are told to cut an inch or so off the bottom of the stems and then put it in water with some plant food added.

This process of cutting the stems off the ends of cut flowers has never logically made sense to me. Neither has it ever made sense to me to cut vines and other plants way back. Pruning of vines is an even more drastic cutting back process than just cutting off the ends of the stems of cut flowers. In fact, when completed, the vine branch can appear to be dead. This pruning is a necessary and a good thing to do, however. In fact, because the branch is attached to the vine, it can grow to be productive, new, and beautiful once again.

This is also true in regards to the cutting or hurtful aspects and experiences of life. Care-giving can often become very challenging and overwhelming. It can be discouraging and hurt us emotionally at times as we see our loved ones deteriorate in their health. Just as we may wonder why it is necessary for a plant to be cut way back, it often is puzzling to understand why we have to undergo these painfully cutting experiences of life.

Yet during my very difficult care-giving years and during my grief since my husband's death, I know the Lord has been shaping my character and drawing me closer to Him. He is also cutting away attitudes and fears that are not appropriate and making me more dependent on Him. Like cut flowers and like a branch on a vine which has been cut back, I can grow into something beautiful and productive because of this pruning in my life. As flowers need plant food, I also have to feed on God's Word for this to take place.

The branch on the vine cannot grow into something beautiful again unless it is attached to the vine. I also cannot grow into something beautiful unless I am attached to the Vine, the Lord Jesus. This is spoken of in John 15.

Dear Christian caregiver, the pruning that takes place in the difficult moments of care-giving — and in life in general — hurts. It is okay to acknowledge that it hurts. You are not alone, however; if you are attached to the Living Vine, Jesus Christ. You will be okay. Not only will you be okay, but you will flourish! Remind yourself of this when the dark moments come.

Adjusting to a New "Normal"

$\mathcal{A}$s I have mentioned several times, my husband had a devastating neurological disease called Multiple Systems Atrophy type C. He was initially diagnosed with this in April of 2006, and a more definite diagnosis was given in the summer/fall of 2006 at Mayo Clinic.

For some time after his diagnosis, my husband continued to work. In fact, he probably continued to work longer than was really safe. The declines continued to come, however. After quitting work, he gradually went from a cane to a walker and finally to a wheel chair. One day, I was looking back at some of my journal posts from May of 2009 and May of 2010. In May of 2009, I was lamenting the fact that my husband needed to graduate to a wheelchair. In May of 2010, sadness filled my heart in recognition of the fact that he needed to have assistance getting into bed. Just a few months later, I needed to use a lift to make transfers with him.

When my husband began needing assistance into bed at night, I wrote the following: "We are adjusting to working together to get him into bed in the evening. That is not the most difficult part. The most difficult part is adjusting to a new 'normal.' It is realizing that we are taking another step back." It was also difficult having to prompt my husband each step of the way when making transfers. It seemed as if his brain was having a problem conveying the message to his body to take the next action.

Each step backwards was so difficult emotionally. Sometimes I felt emotionally at the end of my rope. I hated what the future likely held for my husband and me in regards to the progression of his disease. I hated the adjusting to new norms which were moving rapidly and constantly downward. Sometimes I feared what the future held. We were dealing with a terrible disease. When I was afraid or angry or discouraged, however, I tried to remember that the Lord held my future. I know I was guided step by step.

My husband entered his eternal home on January 2, 2011. He is free from his disease. I miss him so much, but I know who still holds my future. Dear Christian caregiver, trust that God holds the future for you and your loved one also. The way ahead may be difficult, but He will be with you step by step.

Conflicting Emotions
and Blessings

I scribed the following words in early June of 2010, about seven months before my husband's death:

My heart is filled with so many conflicting emotions tonight. I feel burdened by the fact that I know we have taken another step backwards in my husband's disease. I now have to help him every time he goes to the bathroom so we don't endanger him of falling, and I am now helping him into bed.

This decline in my husband's health also means I have to get up in the middle of the night if he has to use the bathroom. It means more fatigue for me. It further means I can't leave him for as long during the daytime. This is discouraging to me. I so tire of the adjustments to new changes and seeking new solutions. Sometimes I wonder how long it will be before I can no longer take care of him. Years? Months?

I still have so many blessings all around me, however. As I am writing this, I can hear the twitter of birds outside my window. I am blessed each day by the perennials around our new home, which have been coming out one at a time. Since I don't know the names of many of the flowers, it has been a joy seeing new, beautiful flowers popping out. They are like little gifts from God assuring me of His love. God also assures me in the Bible that He will always be with me.

I was blessed the other day by my sister-in-law taking my husband out for a drive and giving me some alone time at home. I was blessed today in church. I am blessed with the knowledge that we will be getting some in-home therapy for my husband scheduled to start tomorrow.

Lord, help me just to trust, just to rest, just to release. Help me not to worry so much about the ending of the story, for it ultimately will be good. Help me to enjoy and revel in the daily blessings, even in the midst of hard times.

Dear caregiver, the challenges of care-giving for a loved one can be so very emotionally, physically, and even spiritually challenging. The heartaches of the declines in the health of your loved one over which you have no ultimate control is so discouraging. Remember, however, dear caregiver, that the Lord is with you each step of the way. Also, in the midst of the heartaches, look for the wonders and blessings. They are always there, and it will help you get through the pain of the tough times.

Words of Affirmation

*F*amily care-giving demands huge sacrifices emotionally, spiritually, and physically from the caregiver. At the same time, it is not often affirmed and recognized by society. Sometimes even the caregiver's loved one does not affirm or acknowledge the love sacrifices that are being made for him or her. They often are not able to do this because they themselves are so overwhelmed with their disease. In the spring of 2009, in the midst of my husband's neurological disease, I wrote the following words:

The other day I took one of those Facebook quizzes. I am never big on these quizzes, because they appear to be a bit of a hoax. The quiz I took this time, however, seemed to match my reality pretty closely. The name of the quiz was "What is Your Love Language?" It said my love language was words of affirmation.

Before my husband's illness, he would tell me I was beautiful, and he would often call me "his favorite wife." It became a standing source of teasing between us, because my reply would always be, "How many wives do you have?" My husband was always good about giving loving cards on special occasions also. So much of that verbal affirmation is gone now. My husband's speech is so poor that basic communication between us is difficult. I also miss the basic bouncing of ideas between us. I miss the verbal exchange.

A day or so ago, I read a devotional in my care-giving devotional book about the importance of God's affirmation of His love for us and His delight in us, His children. Knowing this is a source of comfort to me more than knowing what I do in my care-giving role has a purpose and meaning. I need to feel affirmed as *me* and not just as my role as a caregiver.

Dear Christian caregiver, the world may not recognize what you do. The loved one for whom you are caring may not always be able to recognize and acknowledge what you do. God, however, does see what you do for your loved one. You are doing noble work, dear caregiver. God also delights in you and loves you just as you are! (Check out Zephaniah 3:17 in the Old Testament of the Bible!)

Fiery Arrows

*A*s a caregiver, do you ever feel as if you are being bombarded by the "fiery arrows" of negative emotions? (Ephesians 6:16) Negative emotions can so easily spring up in the midst of care-giving chaos and heartache.

On June 9, 2009, while caring for my husband, I wrote the following words:

> It is so easy to allow myself to get bogged down with discouragement, impatience, and some-times anger. I realize I need to fight those "fiery arrows." There is still so much for which to be thankful. I need to concentrate on that.

Then on June 23, 2009, I scribed these words:

The future is unknown and feels scary for Wayne and me, but I do know the Lord who holds the future. I need to focus on that and on the fact that I know my Lord will always be with me.

One way caregivers can fight the "fiery arrows" of negative emotions is by remembering the good things that still are present in their lives. Care-giving can be physically, emotionally, and spiritually draining. There are always blessings in one's life, however. We need to look for them and be grateful for them. We also need to look for the wonders of God's work and guidance in our lives. If we look for these things, we will find them. If we look for these things, it will also help to soothe the negative emotions.

Caring for someone with a terminal or serious disease can be frightening at times. This is because the future is so uncertain. Hence, fear and other negative emotions are able to quickly surface. It is wise to take things one day and one step at a time. It is also wise to leave the future in the hands of the Lord. Caregivers tend to be great advocates for their loved ones. In the end, however, caregivers need to remember that they are not in control. God alone holds their futures and the futures of their loved ones. In the measure caregivers can rest in the Lord's care, the negative emotions will be soothed.

As a caregiver for my husband, I found that fighting the "fiery arrows" of negative emotions was a constant struggle. If it were not for my faith, I would not have been able to persevere. My faith and knowing that God was in control made all the difference. The promises in God's Word that He would always be with me soothed my fears and other negative emotions. Finally, the weapon of prayer and looking for God's working in my life was a big help in fighting those "fiery arrows."

Dear Christian caregiver, remember that emotions (negative or otherwise) are just feelings. Feelings are not necessarily based on truth. Only God's Word and resting on your faith in God is the source of truth. Look for the blessings in your life, and rest in His truth.

Replace

The emotional burdens that accompany caring for a loved one can be heavy at times. On July 12, 2010, in the midst of my days caring for my husband, I wrote the following:

> I am seeking this month to replace carrying around my emotional burdens with consciously seeking to release them to God in prayer. Every time a negative emotion comes up (and they have continued to come up), I have resolved to take a deep breath and release them or give them to God. Like one releases a balloon, I want to continually release these feelings to God.

I am serious enough about this that I have even made a visual of this with my computer print program. My picture is of a kite floating in the air and also of a hot air balloon. I also have the names of emotionally negative feelings that I want released from my life. I think it is helpful to have this resolve and word picture in my mind. I am consciously trying to release the negative emotions as they come up. I also realize, however, that this will be a continual battle, because the negative emotions come up so easily and without warning.

When I think too frequently about how much my husband has declined in the last four years, it is still easy to become sad. When I think about his latest transition downward so that he requires my help every time he needs to use the bathroom and all the ramifications of that, it is easy to feel discouraged. When my husband's spends many hours sleeping some days, it is easy to feel lonely, trapped, and frustrated. When I wonder how long I can take care of him before he needs to go to a nursing home, I feel fear and a host of other emotions. Care-giving is demanding enough, however, without carrying around the extra negative emotions. Moreover, my God wants me to release them to Him. He wants me to trust Him.

As I think about my picture, I wonder if the kite or the hot air balloon is a better picture. It would seem the hot air balloon is a better word picture. With the kite, I am still hanging on to the string trying to maintain control. There are things I can and must do as an instrument in God's hands in regards to my husband's health care. Negative emotions and things beyond my control have to be completely released, however.

There are still many negative emotions and sad moments, but I am fighting the fight. I am seeking to release. I call that victory moment by moment. I call that falling down and then getting up again. I call that being a weak human with supernatural help from above, if I just avail myself of it.

Dear Christian Caregiver, what emotional burden can you release today? With what can you replace that emotion? Give it to the Lord, dear caregiver.

Too Much for Me?

$\mathcal{D}$ear family caregiver, have you ever said to yourself, "This is too much for me! I cannot handle the stress and emotional burdens of care-giving for one more day!"? I know I thought those thoughts when I was a caregiver.

One day in the middle of July of 2010, I was feeling very despondent. I was seeing yet again some serious declines in my husband's health. I had been led to believe the life expectancy after diagnosis of his rare neurological disease was six to ten years. Wayne's declines were coming so fast, however, that I felt as if I was always a step behind in keeping up with them. As it turned out, Wayne only lived about four and a half years after his diagnosis and about five and half months after that discouraging day in July of 2010.

On that day in the middle of July, I found myself having a good cry. At that time I hardly ever cried, because I felt I had to stay so strong all the time. So this was a bit rare for me then. First of all, Wayne had been spending a good portion of his time sleeping away his days. Then we had experienced some rather difficult transfers from his wheelchair to the bathroom and back to his wheelchair the day before. I also had recently received some other discouraging news. I was feeling like I could not do this anymore. I was feeling as if it was all too much for me.

Soon after that, I received a card in the mail from my son's family from Iowa. The front of the card read like this, "Nothing that comes your way is too much for you. No matter what it is, God is more than equal to it—you're not, but He is and He lives in you." Wow! Talk about a message from God just when I really needed it. Inside the card was a personal message thanking me for all that I did for Wayne, my son's dad.

Earlier in that same week, I had placed an ad in our local village ad paper for care-giving help for an hour once or twice a week in the evenings to get my husband to the bathroom and into bed. I thought I would be doing well if I received just one reply. Yet that paper came out that same day and I received five replies! I was able to set up with one of the women who responded to come in twice a week, and later three times a week, for an hour each at bedtime. The rates were also very reasonable. So that was another spirit lifter that day. This lady helped me the last months of my husband's life. Also, at the very end, my local son was able to step up and help me.

Those care-giving years were very difficult and emotionally and physically challenging, but God was with me each step of the way. He paved the way. He will pave the way for you also, dear Christian caregiver.

Valuable Lessons Taught

$C$are-giving, by its very nature, tends to teach valuable life lessons. In many ways, care-giving is a grief process for caregivers as they see their loved ones continue to decline. As a caregiver for my husband for over four and one half years, I also found the care-giving experience to be a great teacher, however.

I think care-giving and its challenges teach us that God uses even the difficulties and heartbreak of caregiving for ultimate good. Care-giving (and life in general) is often difficult. Yet we know that God does not waste our sorrows. When we think of Jesus on the cross, we know that eternal life came from that death on the cross. From something as awful as Christ's crucifixion came the best thing that could possibly happen, namely our salvation. So very good things come from very bad things. In the same way, God brings ultimate good out of the heartbreak of care-giving. He uses care-giving to build our character and draw us closer to Him. God never wastes our sorrows.

I think care-giving also teaches us that life is always out of our control. Hence, seeking self-sufficiency is a terrible place to be. Delusions of strength and self-sufficiency will, in fact, hurt us. Caregivers soon realize that the role of care-giving is too big for them in their own strength. Realizing their need for their dependence on the Lord is essential. Acknowledging one's weakness and dependence on the Lord is a good thing. It is a valuable lesson to learn. Care-giving often teaches that lesson.

For a variety of reasons, sometimes others will let us down and not be there when we need them. The Lord, however, will never let us down or betray us. He alone is the One to whom we can go and pour out our hearts and also allow Him to speak to us. The Christian caregiver can speak to the Lord all through the day, at any moment. Care-giving and its difficulties allow the caregiver an opportunity to pray like never before. I do not know what I would have done without the presence of the Lord in my life during those difficult care-giving years. So care-giving teaches us the value of prayer.

Finally, care-giving teaches us that we need the promises of the Bible to sustain us. As a caregiver, I found that it was essential to try to begin every day in God's Word. God's Word contains so many awesome promises of His care, guidance, and presence. Hence, I found the promises of the Bible comforting and necessary in my duties as a caregiver. Care-giving is so very emotionally, physically, and spiritually draining. Without the promises of God's Word, I do not think I could have survived my care-giving days.

Dear Christian caregiver, read God's Word. Study it, meditate on it, memorize it, and internalize it. Christian caregiver, lean on the Lord and on His promises in the Bible; and trust that He will bring good out of the chaos of care-giving.

Other Life Lessons Taught

*I*n my last meditation, we talked about some of the life lessons taught by care-giving. There are so many lessons a caregiver can learn through his or her experience with care-giving that it cannot be contained in just one entry, however. I am sure we could fill many pages talking about life lessons learned while being a caregiver.

Care-giving, by its nature, teaches what is important and what is not important. It teaches that frivolous mate-rial things are *not* important. Family and relationships *are* important. As a caregiver, I was also reminded that my treasures did not lie in earthly things but in heavenly things. My faith in my Lord God and my relationship with Him was and is alone of supreme value. Care-giving, because of its challenges and sometimes heartaches, further tested my beliefs between what I said I believed and what I really believed in regards to my faith in my Lord.

Another important truth learned from care-giving is that God is good. Circumstances may be bad, but God is good. God is the very definition and essence of goodness. He proved that by sending His son on the cross. Thus, He can help and guide caregivers who are struggling to make their way through the maze of making impossible and confusing decisions about their loved ones' care. He can help caregivers who are struggling to keep emotional and spiritual equilibrium in the midst of the heartaches of seeing their loved ones decline in their health.

Care-giving further teaches that joy can coexist in the midst of the heartaches and grief that often accompany care-giving. This is because joy is not based on circumstances which are favorable or perfect. Rather, it is based on a relationship with the Lord.

Finally, care-giving teaches that God is sovereign and in control. Nothing happens to a Christian caregiver (or his or her loved one) that is not filtered through God's love. This is true even in the heartbreaking events which often accompany care-giving. When this truth is accepted, it a soft place to land when overwhelmed with care-giving difficulties or life's difficulties in general.

Knowing I could trust that God loved me and was in control in the midst of the confusion and grief of my husband's disease and eventual death made and continues to make all the difference in the world. Dear Christian caregiver, never forget that the Lord loves you; and He is good. He is in control.

Heartaches and Hope

As I have mentioned before my husband, Wayne, had a devastating and fast moving rare neurological disease called Multiple Systems Atrophy type C. The last couple years of his life in particular were very difficult.

At various times in Wayne's illness, we tried physical therapy. By the summer of 2010, things were becoming increasingly difficult, however. In August of 2010 I wrote the following:

Has our life been reduced to therapy three times a week and sleep days in between to recover? It gets a little discouraging. I am trying to remember the blessings tonight, and there are many. I can't help but feel a little discouraged tonight, however. I don't think I could handle this, if I did not have my Lord on my side and holding my future. I know there is purpose in all this, even though it is sometimes hard to see.

Transfers were also becoming increasingly difficult. I often had to direct Wayne each step of the way. At the very end of his life I had to use a lift with him. About a year and a half before Wayne's death, I also had to begin to thicken his liquids. We discovered that Wayne now had to have all of his liquids thickened to nectar consistency to help prevent them from slipping down too quickly and getting into his wind pipe and/or lungs.

When one has a disability and disease like my husband had, it changes everything. This was especially clear to me on our last wedding anniversary together. In past years, we would have tried to go to a special restaurant for our anniversary. That year I ordered at a fast food place and we ate in the car. Because of my husband's issues (and so I could get some sleep), we also each went to our separate beds that night. So our anniversary seemed somewhat symbolic of what was now so different in our relationship. We both loved each other, but it seemed so different from the husband-wife relationship we had once enjoyed.

Yes, there were moments of enjoyment yet during those years. We enjoyed spending time with our children and our grandchildren. We also enjoyed a couple of long weekend trips with my siblings, but even those moments were overshadowed to some extent with his disability. There were so many issues with Wayne's disease that made life a constant struggle.

Living those care-giving years was very difficult. Remembering them is also difficult. Through all the heartache, however, I learned that my hope and help could only be found in the Lord. He was and is a faithful God. Whatever your heartaches, turn to the Lord, dear caregiver.

Remember the Love

One day in August of 2010, a few months before my husband's death and in the midst of the chaos of care-giving, I was having a good day. The weather was beautiful and free of all the heat and humidity we had been experiencing. Secondly, my husband was having a good day and he had experienced a good therapy session. Finally, I had just finished reading some letters that my husband and I had written to each other in 1970 and 1971 before we were married.

Wayne and I met and dated from April of 1970 to the end of the school year, and then we dated again in the next school year until our marriage on July 30, 1971. I was a teacher then, and I went home to my parent's house during the summers. Wayne went to summer camp for the Army Reserves both summers. The first summer, I also spent six weeks involved in a summer mission program, and the second summer I was at my parent's home preparing for our wedding in my hometown and state while he was getting things squared away in Wisconsin for our first home.

On that particular August day in 2010, I was inspired to read our love letters which we had written to each other those two summers when we were separated while dating. It proved a real joy to me to reread those letters that day, and I found myself smiling often. Those letters reminded me that the first summer Wayne was more confident of his feelings for me than I was for him. I knew I liked him, but I needed to be certain about love and marriage. The next summer when we were corresponding, we were engaged and both of us were sure of our love for each other. It was fun to reread about our young love.

I thought that rereading these old letters might make me feel a little sad, thinking back to those days and comparing it with the life we were now living dealing with Wayne's neurological condition. I guess it did a little. We had matured so much since those early days, however, and I was glad for that growth in maturity. I actually probably felt more saddened about no longer being able to do some of the fun things we had done together during our "empty nest" years.

So reading those letters put a smile on my face that day. It reminded me of what was, and it reminded me of the beginning of our love. I love reading inspirational (Christian) romance books as a way to relax. Reading these letters was a little like that, except it was my story. That day, I had a smile on my face.

Dear Christian caregiver, terminal disease can change the relationship a caregiver has with his or loved one who is ill. Take time often to remember the love that was and still exists. It will lighten the load.

His Faithfulness

*I*t was August 24, 2010. It was my birthday. Family members were at our house to celebrate that night. Earlier in the day we had received a mobility chair for Wayne. It was perhaps a sign of things to come. Wayne's declines came fast and furious in the next four months, and the emotional anguish and stress proved heavy during that time.

Something else happened on the memorable day in August, however. One of my family members called to me to come outside to look at a beautiful rainbow that had appeared in the sky. That rainbow was indeed awesome! I could not remember seeing such a beautiful and full rainbow across the whole sky like that rainbow.

That rainbow that day felt like a special birthday present to me from God Himself. It was a reminder to me of the faithfulness of my God, a God who said to me and continues to say to me that He will never leave me or forsake me. (Hebrews 13:5b in the Bible)

God has indeed proven Himself faithful in those months since that August day in 2010. The next few months in 2010, as I have alluded to before, were very stressful and discouraging as my husband's health deteriorated at an alarming rate. God provided strength and resources all along the way, however. Wayne entered Heaven on January 2, 2011. He was free from the body in which he had been trapped and could now enjoy the Lord's presence forever. For me, it was the beginning of a difficult grief journey. Through it all, however, the Lord has taught me so much about His faithfulness and my need to be dependent on Him. It has also deepened my relationship with the Lord and made me a more compassionate person.

Dear Christian caregiver, God never promises to give us a life without problems and trials. Care-giving for someone with a serious illness is one of life's deepest trials. I know this is true, because I walked that path. God, however, has promised to walk with us through life's heartaches. He has promised to be faithful. Look for His wonders, dear caregiver. Rest in His faithfulness.

Mixture of Joy and Sorrows

*L*ife can be such a mixture of joys and sorrows. Even in our most difficult moments, there is always something for which we can be thankful. Care-giving for a family member with a terminal illness can be overwhelming. It helps to also remember the blessings in one's life, however. On September 12, 2009, in the midst of my care-giving days, I scribed some of my thoughts on this subject. Perhaps you can relate, dear caregiver. I wrote the following words on that day:

Care-giving, like the weather, always has its ups and downs. Some days feel stormy, and on those days I feel I can't do it anymore. On other days life tends to take on a certain rhythm and

193

pattern and is workable. Life always tends to be a mixture of joys and sorrows. I am joyful in my faith and in my relationship with my Lord. I am thankful that I know He is always with me. It is difficult living with the reality of my husband's disease, however. I am happy that the struggles of life are making me stronger in my character, in my faith, and as a person. I struggle with the fact, however, that it sometimes has to be so emotionally exhausting; and I wonder why life has to be so difficult.

I am happy that my husband seems to be gaining much more physical strength through his therapy. I mourn the fact, however, that his balance issues remain and that he is beginning to hang to the side in a more pronounced way when sitting in his wheelchair. I find joy in the times we spend with our grandchildren and in our enjoyable times with family. My joys are definitely better because of the sorrows.

I do weary of being responsible for so many decisions, however. When we bought a different vehicle this summer I did all the talking and dealing. When there are telephone calls to be made or problems to be solved, it is I who has to take charge. Soon we will have some major insurance issues to consider. That will be mainly my responsibility. We may have a chance to move from our apartment to a condo. There is a condo in our price range available, but all the things to think about in regards to such a possibility are a bit overwhelming.

I love the good times my husband and I still have together, but I miss the way things used to be. I miss the times when my husband took more responsibility for these types of things and decisions. I miss the person my husband used to be. Lord, help me choose joy and gratitude today. Continue to direct my path, as You have in the past.

Dear Christian caregiver, never forget that the Lord is always with you each step of the way. Let Him be your source of strength, comfort, and joy as you deal with the heartaches and sorrows of care-giving.

Emotional Roller Coaster

September of 2010 proved to be emotionally draining in many ways for me as a caregiver. It was the beginning of many exceptionally stressful days and the prelude to my husband's death on January 2, 2011. It was an emotional roller coaster month.

On September 2, 2010, my mother-in-law passed away in the early morning. She was 88 years old and, except for the last two years of her life when she was fighting ovarian cancer, she had lived a healthy life. It was difficult to say good-bye to her, but we knew she was now free of all sadness and sickness and was experiencing only pure joy with her Lord. We were happy for her.

During the week of my mother-in-law's funeral, there were the joyful highs of having all three of our sons' families at our home together for the first time in three years. My husband, Wayne, also had a great day on the Sunday we were altogether. I hadn't seen him smile that much in a long time. Yet, as great as it was to have family around, there was a lot of stress in having a household of people along with taking care of my husband's needs.

There were also the stresses and lows of Wayne having a very difficult day both the day before his mother's funeral and again on the day after the funeral. On those days, he did not function at all well and transfers were very difficult. There was also the stress of wondering if Wayne would be able to function well on the day of the funeral. (He did function well on that day, and so he was able to attend the funeral.)

In the days and weeks after my mother-in-law's funeral and after our children's families returned to their own homes, there continued to be a whirlwind of emotions swirling around in my heart. My mother-in-law's decline and death and its accompanying grief tended to blend with my grief connected with my husband's illness and decline.

By September of 2010, the constant ups and downs of my husband's disease really became draining. So often, Wayne would have one or two relatively good days followed by a "crash" day where he slept most of the day. These crash days sometimes also involved difficultly in managing his transfers to the bathroom, bed, the car, etc. His brain was simply having increased difficulty processing and making the moves he needed to make.

So those weeks in September of 2010 consisted of emotions swinging from one extreme to another. I felt stress because of all the emotions and all that had occurred. I do not know how I would have gotten through those days without the Lord. Dear Christian caregiver, lean on the Lord in those emotional roller coaster days.

Finding an Oasis

*B*ecause care-giving for a family member can be so intense, it is important to take little breaks and to seek an occasional oasis from care-giving. Both in October of 2009 and 2010, my husband and I went away for a few days to the Wisconsin Dells with my son's family. My son's family went to great lengths, including taking out the back seat of their van, to accommodate my husband's mobility equipment or a special chair.

We also always enjoyed our Thursday night suppers at my son's family home. As long as I was able with my husband's deteriorating health, I also took occasional substitute teaching days and I helped my daughter-in-law with home schooling our local granddaughters on

Wednesday mornings. I further sang in the church choir and attended woman's Sunday school.

In addition to this, I attended some concerts with a group of ladies. About half a year before my husband died, I hired a CNA to help me a few nights a week so I could attend these occasional concerts. I found when I had these little breaks from care-giving, I was better able to keep things in perspective and keep my spirits up.

Dear caregiver, care-giving for a loved one is so intense and stressful that it is important that you find an occasional oasis from your care-giving. If you are not able to leave your loved one alone even for brief periods of time, bring in someone else to stay with your loved one from time to time. Also, plan and make a little oasis or spot in your home where you can retreat and regroup. Finally, I found I needed to rise earlier than my husband every morning to spend time with the Lord in prayer and Scripture reading. Finding these moments of oasis are essential to your emotional and spiritual well-being, dear caregiver.

Life's Unexpected Twists and Turns

*B*y early October of 2010, a few months before my husband's death, my stress level was often extremely high. Things seemed to be getting more and more difficult in caring for Wayne. I knew God was guiding me. I had seen that over and over, but it was still difficult.

In early October of 2010, I wrote:

Frankly, there are days when I am not sure how much longer I can do this. However, it seems like every time I am at the end of my rope, some other help falls into place. I will have to keep trusting. I realistically need to also at least look into all the options, including possible nursing homes in the future. I hope to avoid nursing homes if at all possible, but I may not have a choice.

Then by the middle of October in 2010, life took some fairly rapidly developing twists and turns in just one week's time. My husband's motor and processing skills rapidly became increasing more limited, and my husband's transfers became increasingly difficult. I was becoming overwhelmingly concerned, and I was feeling that I could not handle my husband's needs any longer. In the midst of all this, my son had lost his job. So in a way, we had two families in crisis.

After somebody talked with me at church on a particular Sunday morning around that time showing concern for my well-being in all this, I decided to have a talk with my son and his wife. I told them that I was getting to the end of my strength in physically handling my husband and that I needed to at least check out nursing homes as a undesired but possible option. My son had already started helping me on nights when my CNA lady did not come. I felt that even that was not enough, however, as I still was handling the days alone at that time.

The upshot of all this was that my son decided (since he was not working) he would come four times a day to help me with transfers to the bathroom, etc.. We now had a scheduled plan for this. The idea was that this would buy me time to at least check out other options.

This was definitely God's timing. A few months after Wayne's passing on to Heaven, my son found a new job (another story of God's mercy and grace). In the meantime, God provided me with the help I needed as Wayne's caregiver. It was such a spirit lifter. My son and I were able to care for my husband's needs until the day of his death, and my heart's desire of avoiding putting Wayne in a nursing home was fulfilled.

I would not want to relive those difficult care-giving days, especially the last few months. In fact, even remembering those days is difficult. God was with me through it all, however. He always provided. He will provide for you also, dear caregiver.

The Caregiver's Race

*L*iving life on this earth, in many ways, is like running a race. In fact, the Bible refers to our lives as a race which must be run with perseverance. I think this is especially true for caregivers. Care-giving for a family member with a terminal or long-term illness involves a determination and perseverance not found in many other of life's experiences.

Running the care-giving race requires energy. It is demanding and emotionally and physically exhausting. It is a race which is never ending. To run this race successfully, caregivers need to rely on God Himself to supply them with the energy and strength to carry on day after day. Caregivers often feel low in energy, but God has promised to supply the strength to continue.

It is also so important for caregivers to feed on God's Word, so that they will have the spiritual nutrients to continue the exhausting care-giving race in which they are participating.

As I mentioned before, running the care-giving race also requires perseverance. It requires a consistent determination to keep going even when tired or when uncertain where the road ahead will lead. This race can also feel very lonely to caregivers. As a caregiver for my husband with a long term terminal illness, I so remember those feelings of fatigue. I also remember those feelings of fear and uncertainty about the future and the loneliness.

However, the Lord has promised to always be with us in all of life's challenges. As He was with me, He will be with you also, dear Christian caregiver. He will never forsake you. He will help you run your care-giving race with perseverance! Dear Christian caregiver, run the care-giving race keeping your eyes upon the Lord. Do this, for He alone is your source of strength. He will also keep you from quitting the race.

Everybody has a race to run in this life. The caregiver's race is different than other people's races. However, it is the race you have been assigned, dear caregiver. Run it in confidence, trusting that you will be given the strength and energy to persevere.

Keeping your Eyes on the Lord

*A*s we discussed previously, life is like a race. It is often a difficult race filled with obstacles and challenges. It is a race of faith. It is important that we keep our eyes on the Lord Jesus. This is especially true of the care-giving race.

Dear Christian caregiver, keep your eyes on Jesus and not on others as you run with faith the care-giving race. If you look around at others, it will discourage and distract you. If you concentrate on another's race, it may seem to you that their life is much easier than your life. First of all, you do not know the struggles they may be facing. Secondly, it may cause envy in your heart. God has assigned you the race that is meant for you, and that is the care-giving race. Or perhaps if you concentrate on others, you may see others who seem to be "holding it together" better than you are. Again, you do not know their struggles. Concentrating on others will only distract and discourage. It will hinder you. Concentrate on the Lord instead.

Also, dear caregiver, do not look inward. If you focus on your limited resources and strength and your own issues, you will become very discouraged. You may even want to give up. The truth is that we are very weak in ourselves. We are totally dependent on the Lord. I remember those days during my care-giving years when I felt as if I could not go on one more day. That was a good place to be, because it made me realize that I was totally dependent on the Lord. Do not look inward, dear caregiver. Look to the Lord.

Finally, dear caregiver, do not look back. It is tempting during care-giving days to look back with longing to the way things used to be. As I saw my husband deteriorate before my eyes, step by step, I grieved each step backwards. I also sometimes longed for days past. That really serves no useful purpose, however, except to discourage and impede.

Dear caregiver, God has assigned you the difficult but vitally significant job of family care-giving. Trust Him to give you the strength to run your care-giving race, and run that race with your eyes focused on the Lord. Don't look back. Focus on Him.

The Lord Will Provide

One of the most discouraging aspects of care-giving for family members with a terminal illness is witnessing the continual deterioration of their bodies. When my husband was first diagnosed with his neurological disease (Multiple Systems Atrophy type C) in 2006, he was still able to work for over a year. After he quit working, he gradually moved from a cane to a walker to a wheelchair, and then finally I had to use a lift with him the last months of his life.

The last months and perhaps weeks of my husband's life, the progression in his disease seemed to take more rapid dives downward. One good thing at that time was that I was able to rent a sit-to-stand lift. Someone from the office of aging and disability told me about this possibility, and so I pursued it. So in late October of 2010, my son and I went to take a look at this sit-to-stand lift at the Home Care Resources store in a local town. A few days later, the lift was delivered.

It took me a couple weeks and a couple of demonstrations to begin to feel comfortable using this product. After I had all my questions answered about the proper use of the product and had practiced using it, I felt fairly comfortable using it. With the lift, I could get my husband transported from one of his chairs to the toilet, to bed, etc. right on target. It was awkward using this lift, and it involved some heavy pushing. It was doable, however.

Those days were difficult, but when I look back I am amazed at God's provision step by step. I am amazed that God provided this lift so that I could keep Wayne out of the nursing home. I am amazed that I learned to use this device by God's grace. I am amazed that God provided my CNA lady, who helped some evenings, and my son to help me during those last months. My house at that time began to look like a nursing home with all the disability equipment standing around, but the Lord provided.

God never promises us a life free from trials. He does promise to be with us each step of the way, however. I have a picture in my kitchen which says, "The Lord Provides." He surely does provide. Whatever heartaches and challenges you are undergoing, dear Christian caregiver, know that the Lord is indeed with you step by step. He will provide.

Never Been This Way Before

*D*ear caregiver, do you weary of the constant changes in your loved one's health? If one's loved one faces a disease from which there is a possible cure, one continues to hope for their recovery. It is difficult going through those days, but there is hope for better days ahead. When the loved one's disease is incurable and the declines are persistent, one enters an even more difficult sphere. As a caregiver, I so remember dreading the next decline in my husband's health. Would I be able to handle his next decline physically and emotionally?

In the book of Joshua in the Old Testament, God's Old Testament people (the Israelites) were about to enter the land that God had promised them many years before. To be able to enter this new land, however, a huge body of God's people had to cross the Jordan River. It would take a miracle for God's people to safely cross the Jordan River, but our Lord God specializes in the impossible.

The officers of God's people told them that when they saw the ark of the covenant of the Lord their God and the Levites who were carrying the ark, they were to move out from their positions and follow the ark. Then they would know which way to go, since they had never been that way before (Joshua 3:3b-4a). The ark was a symbol of the Lord's presence among them. Only if God's people did this would they know which way to go and what to do next, for this was new and foreign territory to them.

As a caregiver, I too had never been that way before. I had never encountered a similar situation or been in the same place in my life. It was a scary place to be. So I also had to keep my eyes focused on the Lord, and I had to follow His leading. Each new day is a new day given to us by the hand of the Lord. When we awaken in the morning, we do not know what new experiences we may face that day. This is especially true for family caregivers.

Every day and moment of our lives is known and planned by the Lord, however. He knows and understands the joys and heartaches caregivers face today and in all the tomorrows which may lie ahead. Caregivers must trust that the Lord will safely lead them each and every day as they keep their eyes focused on Him and follow Him. Before they crossed the Jordan River their leader, Joshua, told God's Old Testament people to consecrate themselves; for the next day the Lord was going to do amazing things among them (Joshua 3:5). The Lord will do amazing things in our lives also, if we trust and follow Him.

In Joshua 3, the waters did not divide while God's people were still in camp or even as they were marching towards the Jordan River. Only when the leaders and people stepped out into the water in faith were God's people able to safely cross the Jordan River! (Joshua 3:15b-16.) Dear caregiver, you may sometimes feel hopeless and even desperate in your care-giving experience. At times like these, commit your needs and desperate situations to the Lord. Like God's Old Testament people, step out in faith. Trust that the Lord will see you through the seemingly impossible Jordan Rivers of your life. The Lord has our lives in His control, and we can trust and follow His leading!

Waves

I scribed the following words in late November of 2010, while caring for my husband. Perhaps you can relate, dear caregiver:

Yesterday, I was awestruck by the beautiful sunrise. First, there were the beautiful pinks coming forth all across the sky, and then the gradual yellows as the early morning sun rose into view. Waves of joy and gratitude for God's faithfulness surfaced in my heart.

Other kinds of waves hit me at times also, however. These are waves of sadness. I really believe my care-giving life has meaning, and I believe there is a purpose and a definite plan for my life through the struggles of care-giving. There are also definite blessings that have come as a direct result of the whole care-giving experience. This does not erase the fact, however, that I am slowly losing the life I once had with my husband. I am slowly losing my best friend. Also, there are so many physical challenges and other emotional challenges with the whole care-giving experience.

Hence, I sometimes have these waves of sadness that hit me. Sometimes it is right in the middle of joyful or pleasant moments and experiences. Recently, it hit me when I was ready to enter a church service. I think that may be because I miss the fact that we were able to attend church together in the past. Today, my son volunteered to give me some time away while he took care of my husband's needs. I enjoyed that very much, but there was a moment or two even then that I felt this wave of sadness come over me. Sometimes I feel it when I first wake up in the morning. I am really struggling for acceptance and gratitude. I believe I have grown some in this area. It is a strange thing, however; this coexistence of waves of joy with waves of sadnes.

Dear Christian caregiver, know that the Lord is with you in the waves of joy and in the waves of sadness. He has promised to never leave you or forsake you. Rest in that, dear caregiver.

Be Conscious of His Presence

ear Christian caregiver, it is vitally important that you stay conscious of the Lord's presence step by step throughout your day. The Lord's presence with you is both a protection and a promise. He will always be with you, and He will never leave you. Go gently through each day, keeping your eyes on the Lord. He will open up the path that He has planned for you step by step. Just trust Him along the way. This is the way to not only survival in your care-giving walk, but also to peace.

Life as a family caregiver is overwhelming at times. The challenges and difficulties are numerous. The promise of the Lord's constant presence is a protection against the pitfalls of despair and self-pity. It is also a protection against worry about the future. When you think about your future and the future of your loved one, envision the Lord in that future because the Lord has promised to always be with you. Keep your eyes focused on the Lord.

Trust God enough to not strive to control or predict the future, dear caregiver. When you try to project your life and your loved one's life too far into the future, you are seeking to be self-sufficient. This will not work. Instead, daily refresh yourself in God's Holy Word, the Bible. Spend time in prayer. Take time to be still in His presence. We all desperately need His help.

Seek to live in the present, dear caregiver, depending on the Lord alone for each moment. I remember as a caregiver feeling so inadequate. That was actually a true assessment. The other fact we must remember, however, is that God has abundantly promised to be our strength. He has abundantly promised to supply all our needs.

Care-giving is so overwhelming that there is no way that I could have handled it without the Lord's strength and presence in my life. You cannot handle your care-giving role alone either, dear caregiver. The truth we all

221

need to acknowledge is that we need the Lord's help with everything. Don't divide your life, dear caregiver, into things you feel you can handle yourself and things for which you know you need the Lord's help. You and I need His help for every single area of our lives. If we give all our needs to Him, we can walk through life with confidence and peace.

Look to the Lord continually for help in the challenges of family care-giving. You are the God appointed comforter and help for your loved one. You often need comfort yourself, however. When you need comfort, the Lord wants to enfold you in His arms. As you receive His comfort, you will be a better channel of comfort to the loved one for whom you are caring and also perhaps for other people.

Treasure the Moments

*I*n December of 2010 my son, Brian, his wife, and my little granddaughter flew in from London. That year, I had mixed emotions about their upcoming arrival. I was glad to see my son and his wife, and I was excited about getting to interact with my little granddaughter. Their anticipated stay of two weeks was a long time, however. I was very busy taking care of my husband at the time and having people around so much (even family) would be emotionally tiring, even when it was a good time.

It turned out that there were joyful moments, blessed moments, and chaotic moments that year. My son from London, his wife, and their two-year-old little girl were here from December 13 to December 27. My son from

Iowa, his wife, and their two daughters were also here from the Wednesday night before Christmas to Sunday the 26th. Our local son, his wife, and their four children were here part of that time, especially on Christmas Eve and Christmas Day.

It was wonderful having them all here for Christmas at one time. It had been a long time since that had happened. My husband, Wayne, experienced an exceptionally good day on that Christmas Day. I consider that one of our blessed moments. That truly was a gift from above.

It was a joyful moment when I saw all of my grandchildren sitting around the table eating a snack or playing together downstairs. It was a blessed and joyful moment when all the grandchildren would come in and crawl on bed and give their grandpa a kiss and hug after he was tucked into bed for the night. The blessed moments also came when everyone was considerate of Wayne's schedule and the way things needed to be with him and even helped me with caring for him.

The overwhelming and chaotic moments came when they were all cooking in the kitchen at the same time and asking me where things were. The overwhelming moments came when the clutter starting piling up with having so many people around so much. The overwhelming moments came when I felt as if I needed and wanted to be there for everyone, especially my grandkids, and I still needed to meet my husband's needs. The overwhelming moments also came when it felt as if I was crowded out of my own space, so to speak.

Those moments were the last Christmas my husband spent with us, however. They are moments upon which we can look back and treasure as a family. My husband passed away a little over a week later on January 2, 2011. Treasure all the moments with your loved ones, dear Christian caregiver.

In the Hands of the Lord

On Saturday, January 1, 2011 my husband, Wayne, turned 65. Even though my husband's health had declined significantly, I had no clue that on Sunday morning, January 2, 2011 — one day after his birthday — I would find that my husband had passed away during the night. The process of the disease was supposed to take six to ten years after diagnosis. Wayne lived only four and a half years after diagnosis. I knew that he would pass away some day, however; and I had anticipated that his eventual death would be somewhat easier because of the grieving I had already done. I had been slowly losing him for a long time. I discovered that certainly was not true, however. Death is so final on this earth. He was the love of my life for so many years.

My body reacted to the shock with chills and nausea, with feelings of being tired and wired at the same time, and with feelings of operating on auto pilot. I also found, however, that now I was beginning to release some tears which I could not release during all those years of having to remain strong in my role as caregiver.

I was so happy for my husband. He was released from a body which had trapped him, and he was now in Heaven. I was sad for myself and my family, as we would miss him. I also wondered, "What next?" As difficult as care-giving truly had been, it also had been my purpose for being on this earth for so long. I would have to rediscover a new purpose in the days ahead.

Dear caregiver, you may find this meditation more discouraging than helpful. If so, I apologize. Death, however, may come some day for your loved one. Know, however, that your loved one (as well as you, dear Christian caregiver), are in the hands of the Lord. God says all the days that we and our loved ones are meant to live on this earth are ordained by the Lord God (Psalm 139:16).

Hence, I plead with you to not engage in false guilt during your care-giving days, or in the possible eventual death of your loved one. It is the devil's trick to discourage you. Also, care-giving for a family member can be all consuming. Hence, when it ends a caregiver can have a sense of loss of purpose. I know I did. Be assured that God will use even that to refine you and mature you. Eventually, the Lord will slowly reveal His new purpose for your life, begin to heal you, and begin to add new joy to your life. What will the future bring for you, dear Christian caregiver? No matter what is brings, trust that the Lord will be with you each step of the way. You and your future are in the hands of the Lord, dear Christian caregiver!

Rest in Him

*I*n the book of Job in the Old Testament, we read about a godly man who lost everything he owned and all his children in a series of disasters. As if that was not sufficient suffering, he was afflicted with a horrible disease.

Do you ever wonder, dear Christian caregiver, why God has allowed the illness of the loved one for whom you are caring? Have you ever wondered why you have to go through all the heartaches and challenges of caring for your ill or disabled loved one? Have you ever wondered why you, a child of God, have to endure these trials?

In the book of Job in the Old Testament, Job began to ask these questions. God responded to Job in chapter

42. In effect, God said, "Who are you to question My ways and My plans? Why should you question Me without knowledge, without understanding My wisdom? You have no right to question Me. Your knowledge is too limited to understand My ways. You do not have My power and wisdom." Later, Job said to God that he had spoken of things that were far beyond his understanding. These were things only God could understand, and Job repented of questioning God's ways.

I do not understand why my husband was afflicted with his devastating neurological disease. I do not know why he had to go through the disabilities and indignities of his disease. I do not know why I had to go through all the heartaches of being his caregiver and eventually losing him to death. However, I must trust God that He knew what He was doing, no matter how difficult life became during those years.

The Bible reminds us that we can trust in the Lord, for He never has and never will forsake us. His ways are perfect, even when we do not understand His ways. He is our shield, and we can take refuge in Him. I can trust in Him and not be afraid of what the future holds. Even in difficult times, He is my strength and song.

I do know that I have been strengthened in my faith, and my relationship with the Lord is more precious than ever before because of all that has happened to me. God has been my help and support through it all. I needed and still need to trust in Him alone. I do not understand all God's ways; but I do know He is a wise, faithful, and loving God. I do know that He is worthy of my trust.

Christian caregiver, you do not know what the future holds for you and your loved one; but you do know that the Lord God holds your future. You may not understand His ways, but He asks you to trust Him. His ways are not always your ways, but He knows what He is doing in what He allows in your life. Rest in Him.

Peace in the Needs

$\mathcal{I}$n a past meditation we discussed the "Why?"
questions that sometimes enter our minds in light
of the difficulties that life presents us. We also discussed
this in relationship to the heartaches and challenges
which often accompany family care-giving. We came to
the conclusion that we do not always understand why
God allows certain things in our lives, but we know
that He is much wiser than we are. We need to trust
Him in these things and trust that He is transforming us
into something beautiful for His kingdom through all
these things.

Dear Christian caregiver, God has taken you along
the path of family care-giving. The challenges of care-
giving have heightened your awareness of your need for

the Lord. Family care-giving may have placed you in circumstances which have made your perceived strengths
useless and irrelevant. It may have also made you aware
that your weaknesses are glaringly evident.

This is a good thing which has occurred as a result
of the difficulties of your care-giving experience, dear
Christian caregiver. During these overwhelming, des-
ert-like experiences in your life, you are realizing your
need for dependence on the Lord. This, in turn, has drawn
you closer and closer to Him.

From that dependence on the Lord and closer relationship with Him, perhaps you have discovered a new
peace blossoming in your heart. This peace has come
right in the midst of all the heartaches. You perhaps have
discovered that needing the Lord and depending on Him
is the key to knowing Him in a much more intimate way.
This is the greatest gift you can receive, dear caregiver!

So will you make a sacrifice of praise and thanks for
even these difficult times in your life, dear caregiver?
Know that through these overwhelming challenges, God
is accomplishing His best work both in your life and in
the life of your loved one. Will you trust Him with your

needs in the days ahead? Will you grow in your intimacy with Him? Will you even thank Him for His work in your life? Will you find His peace?

Frustrations and Encouragement

Care-giving for a loved one with a terminal illness is, at best, emotionally and spiritually challenging. On January 28, 2009 in the middle of my care-giving days, I wrote the following words:

> Today I had many feelings of frustration. Frustration at my husband's disease and frustration at my husband for not doing things I think he could do to fight off the speed of the progress of this disease. Mixed with these feelings was a little cabin fever again and feelings of guilt for having feelings of frustration.

Tonight, I do feel better. I went to mid-week services in church. In this case what probably helped me the most, however, was talking with a couple of ladies after the service. Even though they are not going through the exact experiences I am going through, they seemed to be able to empathize with me on many levels. They also assured me of their prayers. The Lord does know who to place in our paths when we need them. Thank you, Lord.

In the frustrations of care-giving, Christian care-givers need to run to the Lord God for strength and encouragement. God sometimes uses other people for that purpose also, however. Dear caregiver, do not be afraid to reach out to others for help and encouragement. Also, remember to thank God for the people He brings into your path which are a source of encouragement.

Finally, there are those who will disappoint you because of their lack of concern and involvement. These people are often people you would think should be the ones who are most helpful in your loved one's care, but they disappoint you in their lack of involvement and concern. Do not concentrate on the disappointments of these people's actions and attitudes; doing that will serve no purpose but to discourage you and bring you down emotionally. God also asks us to forgive those who are not there for us physically and emotionally when we need them. Rather, thank God for those who do step up and help by their words, actions, or prayers. They are truly a gift from God.

Gladness Even
in the Difficult Days

The Bible tells us that we should find joy and be glad for every day given to us by the Lord God (Psalm 118:24). If you are a family care-giver and know the challenges and heartaches that accompany that calling, you may ask yourself how that is possible. How is it possible to find joy in each new day when one sees one's loved one deteriorating in his or her health month by month and sometimes day by day?

I think one way caregivers are able to do this is by remembering that the Lord God created each day. He is with you and present in your day, whether you sense His presence or not. Rejoice in the fact that He understands your needs as a family caregiver, and He knows exactly

238

the emotional and physical toll it is taking on you. He also understands the needs of the loved one for whom you are caring.

Commune with the Lord throughout the day. Tell Him your needs and concerns. He will soothe your pain. Know that you are not in control. Depend on Him. This will lighten your emotional load and your spirit considerably. Doing this does not mean that all the heartaches of care-giving will suddenly disappear, but awareness of the Lord's presence in your life can infuse joy into your most difficult of care-giving days.

Also, the best response to the challenges of a difficult care-giving day is praise and thanks. I remember as a caregiver being challenged to write down each day at least three things for which I was thankful. That little exercise in itself did a lot to change my perspective during those overwhelming days of caring for my husband with a serious neurological disease.

Finally, trust that the Lord has the future — of you as a caregiver and of your loved one — in His hands. God may choose to heal your loved one on this earth. God may, on the other hand, choose to heal your loved one completely by taking him or her to eternity, as He did my husband. Don't spend your energy wondering and worrying about the road ahead. God is in control. Instead, stay in close communion with the Lord. He will guide and pave the way.

Caregivers of Strength

*A*s a caregiver, it is very important that you eat right, exercise when you can, and in general do all you can to maintain your good health. Dear caregiver, you are not able to be of comfort and help to the loved one for whom you are caring if you do not do all in your power to stay healthy yourself. Taking care of yourself physically is so important for you to become a caregiver of strength.

Even more important than your physical health is your emotional and spiritual health. Family care-giving can be emotionally and spiritually draining. That is why it is so important that you maintain your spiritual health through daily prayer and reading the Word of God. If this means you have to get up in the morning before your loved one arises for the day, then that is what you need to do. It is essential to your well-being and for you being a caregiver of strength. Also, throughout the day constantly tune into the presence of God right beside you.

The Bible tells us not to be afraid. Yet is so easy for caregivers to let worries attack them. As a caregiver for my husband, I remember being so afraid of what the future held for my husband and me. The prognosis for his neurological disease was eventual total disability. That was exactly what happened. Satan wants us to despair during these times, and yet the Lord understands our weaknesses in this area. In the midst of the fearsome circumstances, caregivers of strength can show courage because of the Lord's strength in them.

Caregivers of strength know that they are fallible human beings. They know they become impatient at times. They often feel like they are walking in the dark. They often feel as if their whole world could fall apart at any moment. They also know, however, that the Lord will catch them and their loved ones when they fall. Caregivers have no confidence in their own strength, but they avail themselves of the Lord's grace and strength.

Caregivers of strength do not continually look for their own advantage. They often sacrifice their own best interests for the best interests of the loved one for whom they are caring. They also know that they do not have enough strength in themselves for the care-giving journey they are on. They further know with certainty, however, that through the care-giving journey they will become strong by God's grace.

Dear Christian caregiver, this is most likely the most difficult journey you have ever experienced. Trust in the Lord's strength. Rest in Him, and you will be a caregiver of strength!

Ruth, the Caregiver

The name of Ruth in the Old Testament immediately comes to mind as a Biblical example of a caregiver. We often associate Ruth along with her mother-in-law, Naomi, as widows. We remember God's provision for them through His servant, Boaz. There is much comfort in the book of Ruth in the Old Testament for widows. There is much in the book of Ruth to which Christian caregivers can relate as well, however

Ruth's husband died while she was probably a relatively young woman. We do not know if this death of her husband happened suddenly, or if Ruth's husband was sick for a long time before he died. We do not know if Ruth needed to fulfill the role of caregiver for her husband.

We do know for certain, however, that Ruth showed a sweet, care-giving spirit with her mother-in-law.

A number of years before, Ruth's mother-in-law Naomi and her husband Elimelech had moved to Moab because of a famine in their land of Israel. After some time in Moab, Elimelech died. Later, both of Naomi's sons died (one of these sons had been married to Ruth). When Naomi decided to return to Israel, Ruth insisted on going with Naomi in spite of Naomi's urgings to not go with her but to return to the comfort of her familiar homeland.

In a beautiful passage in Ruth 1:16-17, Ruth begged Naomi not to ask her to leave her. She promised Naomi that Naomi's people and God would be her people and God. This, I believe, was a beautiful commitment to God, but it was also a beautiful commitment to Naomi on the part of Ruth. Ruth was willing to sacrifice everything secure in her life to be Naomi's caregiver and provider. Even though Naomi was not ill at the time, she needed the loving care and support that Ruth would give her. We read in the Old Testament book of Ruth how Ruth did all she could to provide for Naomi, in spite of Naomi's initial lack of gratitude and warmth.

You too, dear caregiver, have sacrificed much to be a loving caregiver to your loved one. You have done this even at times when little appreciation was shown in return for your actions. You have most likely not been a perfect caregiver, yet you have persevered in what you felt God was calling you to do. You have been willing to forgo your own comfort because of the love and commitment you have for your loved one.

Dear Christian caregiver, God, our Redeemer (of whom Boaz was a picture), will bless you and protect you as He did Ruth. Your work is so very important, even though it appears overwhelming and hopeless at times. Trust that God will bless you for your efforts through His presence and care on this earth. Most importantly, He is laying up treasures for you in Heaven!

Fighting Discouragement

Satan loves to try to discourage us and rob us of our joy as believers. Satan can never snatch us out of the hand of our Lord God, for we are safe in the hands of the Lord forever. So Satan tries to do the next best thing in his eyes. Satan tries to rob us of our joy and effectiveness as Christians.

As a caregiver, it is so easy to become discouraged. The heartaches of seeing one's loved one suffer and deteriorate in his or her body can be very overwhelming. Even the psalmists in the book of Psalms in the Old Testament often expressed feelings of discouragement. In some cases, they were experiencing deep trials in spite of their present faithfulness to the Lord God. Hence, they sometimes felt abandoned, crushed, and devalued by God.

One strategy for fighting discouragement demonstrated in the Psalms is prayer. Prayer should be our first recourse for help, deliverance, and restoration in times of trouble and challenge. Prayer should also be our first recourse in fighting the discouragement which sometimes accompanies difficult times. Through the avenue of prayer we can gain peace, joy, and relief from discouragement in facing life's challenges.

Another strategy for fighting Satan's attempts to discourage us is a firm confidence in the Lord's directing and unfailing love, kindness, and faithfulness. We must also pray with the psalmists of old for the Lord God's guiding and directing light and truth on our paths throughout this life. If we saturate our lives with prayer and the truths of God's Word, we will have the confidence of the Lord's presence in our lives. We will also have His joy in full and a song in our hearts (Psalm 42:8).

Remembering and praising God for His past mercies among His people and in our own personal lives is another great way to fight Satan's attempts to discourage us. A powerful deterrent to discouragement in present trials and in future challenges is remembering how the Lord God has helped us in the past (Psalm 77:11-12).

Yet another strategy for fighting discouragement is God-directed self-talk (Psalm 42:5 & 11 & Psalm 43:5). Saturating one's mind with God's Holy Word and then verbally reminding oneself of the awesome truths and promises of God's Holy Word is one of the best prescriptions against Satan's discouraging lies.

One final strategy in fighting discouragement is to vow to praise God during our trials and in excited anticipation of the Lord's answers to our prayers and wonders in our lives (Psalm 43:4). May the Lord God's song and joy (not Satan's discouraging lies) reside in you, dear caregiver, and in all of us!

His Abounding Love

*G*od is a God who is abounding in love. Sometimes in the storms of care-giving challenges, it may not feel that way. Feelings do not change the truth of God's unfailing love for you, however, dear caregiver.

If you think of your life as a building, the Lord is your sure foundation, dear caregiver. He is guiding you through the difficult challenges of care-giving. He is guiding you with His wisdom and knowledge when you feel like you are hitting your head against brick walls. Many times when I was a caregiver I felt so alone. Yet I always knew God was with me, and now as I look back I see how He led me each step of the way.

Every building also needs a door. Prayer is the door or access to the very presence of God. So is trust and thankfulness. As we trust in Him with a thankful heart, He will pave the way. Family care-giving is overwhelmingly difficult at times. I know that, dear caregiver, because I lived it. Yet God's presence is with you all the way. You will sense that presence more as you pray to Him and trust Him with a thankful heart.

Every building also needs a security system of some kind. This is to prevent others from coming in and doing damage to property or people. The caregiver's life needs a security system also. That security system is the Word of God. As caregivers listen and wait for God to speak to them through the promises of His Word, they are able to fight off the devil's attempts to discourage them. They are able to rest in the abounding love of the Lord God.

Dear caregiver, there is not even one area of your life that the love of God is not able to reach. God's wide and loving arms are able to reach around any care-giving challenge in your life. He will never leave you or forsake you. His love is deep enough to meet your deepest discouragement as you go about the business of caring for your loved one.

Not only is His love with you, dear caregiver, but so is His all-sufficient power. He can calm your fears. In your own strength it is not possible to face the challenges of family care-giving, but He has promised to give you His strength in you! With His strength in you and with His abounding love surrounding you, dear caregiver, you can do whatever He asks of you. Rest in Him!

Praise the Lord

*F*amily caregivers often face overwhelming physical and emotional struggles as they care for their loved ones. This is especially true if their loved ones have a terminal disease and are deteriorating in their health month by month and sometimes day by day. In many cases, caregivers' dreams for a beautiful future with their loved ones have been shattered. They also often feel weighed down with fears about the future.

Dear Christian caregiver, do not let Satan discourage you by his schemes at times like this. Satan is a liar and he wants you to forget that you are a child of God with the power of God on your side. Satan wants you to forget that you have Christ's resurrection power in you to live for God and carry out your difficult care-giving role. Trust in the Lord. Rest in Him, dear caregiver.

One way caregivers (or anyone, for that matter) can fight Satan's schemes to discourage us is to praise the Lord in the midst of difficulties. It seems to go so against our instincts to praise the Lord during difficult times, but thankfulness takes the sting out of trials and adversity. The chains of discouragement and despair drop behind us when we praise the Lord. I read somewhere recently that if we give thanks to God in spite of our feelings, He in turn gives us joy in spite of our circumstances. We sense God's presence when we are praising Him in a way that we are not able to do in any other way. It is said thanksgiving and praise in our hearts squeezes difficult circumstances until joy oozes out of it. Praise for the Lord gives us glimpses of Heaven, which in turn gives us further reasons to be thankful.

I still remember very vividly those care-giving days when I was taking care of my husband with a rapidly deteriorating neurological disease. Those days were very difficult. This was especially true the last months of his life. It is hard to feel thankful and full of praise in such moments. God asks us to make a SACRIFICE of praise, however, even in those difficult moments. If we do this, we will find peace and joy as we are resting in Him. We may not always understand God's ways, but He does have everything under His control.

Praise the Lord in the midst of all the challenges and difficulties, dear caregiver. It will lift your load.

Easter and the Caregiver

I love Easter best of all the holidays. I love it for its deep spiritual significance. Yet how does Easter relate to family care-giving?

Easter means that the Lord Jesus came to this earth and lived a perfect life for you and me. He later died on the cross to pay the price for our sins, and then He arose again on the third day to prove that He had won over sin and death and Satan. If you and I have accepted his gift of salvation by repentance and faith, we are His children now and for eternity.

Easter also means that Jesus Christ, the Son of God, identifies with your pain and the pain of your loved one, dear caregiver. As you struggle to help your loved one who is perhaps fighting against an incurable disease,

Jesus Christ identifies with you. Having suffered the worst possible pain for us on the cross, He is able to sympathize with our heartaches and weaknesses. He is also an all-powerful Savior to whom we can freely go for grace in our moments of sadness and overwhelming and crushing needs. (Check out Hebrews 4:15-16 in the New Testament.)

Dear Christian caregiver, because of Easter and Christ's sacrifice, you can freely approach God the Father Himself with both your needs and your loved one's needs. You can cry out to Him for help and call Him your "Abba Father," because He considers you His special child (Romans 8:15). Easter also means that when your heart is so weighed down with the heartaches and overwhelming circumstances of family care-giving that you do not even know how to pray, the Holy Spirit will intercede and pray for you! (Romans 8:26.)

Easter for the caregiver means that although you will always face trials and troubles in this world, the Lord Jesus Christ has overcome the world. He is also your source of peace even in the most challenging of times (John 16:33). Even in the overwhelming circumstances of family care-giving and even when we do not understand God's ways in allowing certain things in our lives, God is working for our ultimate good. We are victors in Him! (Romans 8:28 & 37.)

Dear Christian caregiver, my hope for you would be that your loved one is healed on this earth. Whether he or she is healed on this earth or not, however, a child of God is whole and perfect upon entering heaven. No matter what happens in your care-giving situation you too, dear caregiver, will slowly heal emotionally and spiritually. God will always be with you, and joy will return one day. His love for you will never fail. He proved that love for you on the cross. That is the meaning of Easter for the caregiver and for all of us.

Simply Trusting

The Lord God is the caregiver's refuge, source of guidance, and assurance in the difficult challenges of family care-giving. Care-giving is one of the most important avenues of service in the kingdom of God. It also can be a time of despair, discouragement, and bewilderment while making decisions concerning the next wisest step in dealing with the health of the loved one for whom one is caring.

Every caregiver needs to ask the Lord to help and guide him or her through the difficult twists and turns of care-giving. This involves also *trusting* that God will guide step by step through this process. God will not usually let the caregiver see far into the future, but the Lord has promised to lead step by step. He will always walk alongside the caregiver with His sustaining strength. He will be the caregiver's refuge each step of the way.

The caregiver needs to choose to rest in the Lord. A caregiver cannot control the circumstances of their loved one's disease, but they can control their response to the circumstances. That response has to be one of trust in the Lord. When one sees one's loved one deteriorating in health, it is so easy to become discouraged and to become fearful, but the Lord is the source of hope. He has everything under His control. He is worthy of our trust.

There are times when the care-giving situation becomes increasingly desperate and hopeless. This can cause the caregiver to feel brokenhearted and want to give up. Remember, dear caregiver, the Lord is very near to you when you feel this way. God sees your overwhelming situation, and He hears your cry for help. He can and will bring you through this storm in your life. He will hear your every cry and meet your every need. You may not always understand God's ways with you and with your loved one; but He will never leave you nor forsake you, dear caregiver.

The Lord may not heal your loved one on this earth, but the Lord will heal your loved one. As a child of God, even if your loved one's disease is not healed on this earth, your loved one will be completely healed in eternity. No matter what happens, the Lord will heal you too, dear Christian caregiver. He will heal you emotionally and spiritually and teach you valuable lessons about His love and faithfulness in the process. Trust in Him. Rest in Him.

The Prayer Helper
for the Caregiver

As we have said numerous times, care-giving for a loved one with a serious disease is one of life's greatest challenges. Only those who have been or currently are family caregivers truly understand the emotional and physical difficulties associated with care-giving.

In the midst of care-giving responsibilities, it is important to focus on the Lord and to turn to Him in prayer. Sometimes in the overwhelming moments we do not know how to pray about our situations, however. At such times, the Holy Spirit helps us in our prayer life. Romans 8:26 promises us that the Holy Spirit helps us in our weakness. We often do not know what we ought to pray for, but the Holy Spirit Himself intercedes for us in a way that mere words cannot express.

Have you ever tried to pray about your care-giving situation and felt so overwhelmed with some heartache that you did not know how to pray? Have you ever felt that you could not find the words to express in prayer the depths of your feelings and the needs in your heart? God understands our weaknesses and has provided us a helper in our prayer lives. That helper is the Holy Spirit Himself!

The Holy Spirit prays in and through us. He also prays for us, especially during those times when we are too overwhelmed with heartache to find the right words to express our pain to the Lord in prayer. The Holy Spirit understands our sorrows and is our prayer helper. The Holy Spirit Himself pleads and intercedes for us before the Heavenly Father! The Holy Spirit is our perfect intercessor before the Heavenly Father, because He intercedes for God's people in accordance with God's will (Romans 8:27b).

Praise the Lord for His infinite blessings! He is our salvation. He is our source of strength, promise, and hope. He provides for every need in our lives for time and eternity. The Lord provides us the Holy Spirit to help us to live for the Lord and to help us in our weaknesses. Finally, the Lord even provides the Holy Spirit as our prayer helper and advocate! What a glorious God we serve! Praise His name!

Lean on Him

Dear caregiver, the heartaches and difficulties of family care-giving can often be very overwhelming. This time in your life may very well be the most difficult trial that you have faced. It is so very physically, emotionally, and spiritually draining to see one's love one deteriorate in his or her health and to know that one is very limited in what one can do to help that loved one.

Care-giving often teaches in a very vivid way that self-dependence does not work. It certainly made that truth very clear to me when I was a caregiver. Dear caregiver, God wants you to lean on Him. He wants you to trust in Him and acknowledge Him. God wants you to have a heart that rests in His promises. He wants you to believe with absolute certainty that He will teach you and guide you every step of the way down your care-giving path.

Surrender to God's plan for your life right now, dear caregiver, even though it is a very difficult path and a path which you would never have chosen for yourself. Daily lean on and depend on God by relying on His promises in His Holy Word and by prayer. He is the answer and daily provides for you and your loved one's needs.

In fact, dear Christian caregiver, God is using the pressures and challenges of care-giving to produce in you a beautiful Christ-likeness. He is molding you into a precious vessel more suitable for His glory and use. In the process of doing this He is guiding you step by step, increasing your trust in Him, giving you His strength, and providing for you and your loved one in a way that is beyond what you think possible or are able to imagine (Ephesians 3:20). We do not always understand or even agree with God's ways, but we can trust them. We can also trust His love. He loved us enough to send His own Son for us. Can we not also trust Him to provide for us, even in life's most challenging situations?

Dear caregiver, family care-giving is often a difficult road to travel. Yet God is leading you and is with you all the way. Lean on Him, dear caregiver.

Caregivers and
the Names of God

During my post care-giving days, I heard some sermons on the names of God in my church. I found those sermons to be a great blessing and comfort to me. I believe thinking about the meanings for some of the many names for God can be a blessing and source of strength for current caregivers as well.

The Old Testament was originally written in Hebrew, and the New Testament was written in Greek. *Elohim* in Hebrew means the all-powerful, almighty, creator God. *Yahweh* is the personal name for God. Yahweh Elohim is your God, dear Christian caregiver! The all-powerful God of the universe cares about you, and He is with you in the difficulties and challenges of care-giving!

He is also *Yahweh-jireh,* which means the Lord will provide. He will provide for you, dear Christian caregiver, in all the uncertainties and stresses of care-giving. You do not know the future, but He already has the future under His sovereign control. I remember as a caregiver often succumbing to fear and worry. It was difficult to see my husband's health deteriorating before my eyes. As I look back, however, I know the Lord was with me each step of the way.

I read somewhere that worrying is trying to carry tomorrow's load with today's strength. It is trying to carry two days at once. Worrying as a caregiver will not empty tomorrow of its heartaches and challenges. Instead it empties today of its strength. The truth of the matter is that we have no strength in ourselves at all, but we have unlimited strength in God. He is in control. He will provide strength as we need it. Trust in *Yahweh-jireh,* which means the Lord will provide. He is also your *Yahweh-nissi,* which means the Lord is my banner or miracle. Trust in Him to provide, dear caregiver.

Dear Christian caregiver, the Lord is also *Yahweh-sabaoth* which means the Lord of Hosts or the Lord

Almighty or the Sovereign Lord. He is Lord over everything. We are not able to box God in and tell Him what to do. If we submit to Him, however, He who is all powerful and Lord over everything will go before us. He will pave the way for you on the difficult path of care-giving. When you recognize that you can't do this care-giving thing on your own He — the Lord Almighty — is with you, dear caregiver. Trust that He is in control. Rest it with the Lord God, for He also alone is *Yahweh-shalom,* which means the Lord is peace!

Your Treasure
and Your Strength

*D*ear Christian caregiver, the Lord is your treasure and strength in the storm of family care-giving. God may be using the storms of your care-giving days to show you His strength in your weakness as you seek to deal with the overwhelming challenges. Because of your relationship with the Lord, dear Christian caregiver, you can approach God with confidence and freedom for help and strength as you face each new day.

I felt so inadequate for the task of being my husband's caregiver. It was not a role I would have chosen, and I certainly felt unprepared for that role. However, God delights to use unlikely, ordinary, weak people to do His will. When you yield your limitations and even failures to the Lord, dear caregiver, you become a wonderful instrument in the Lord's hand. His strength and not your own will then fill you.

Also, I know of no greater work in the kingdom of Heaven than family care-giving. It is often a thankless job accompanied by grief and perhaps tears as one sees one's loved one's health deteriorate. It is never a pointless role, however. For whatever is done for others is done for the Lord, and it will produce a harvest of blessings and joy in God's perfect timetable.

The family care-giving role is a role that often feels as if it is leading down blind alleys. Christian caregivers, however, can be assured that their Good Shepherd is leading and guiding them each step of the way. The Good Shepherd knows that you are very vulnerable, dear caregiver. Depend on Him for guidance and protection just as lambs follow their shepherd. As your Good Shepherd, He will walk before you and lead you. He is your hope for today as you face your care-giving challenges. He is also your hope and the hope of your loved one for the future! He is your treasure and your strength, dear Christian caregiver!

Focus on the Lord
in the Storms

As a caregiver, perhaps your dreams for the life you hoped to share with your loved one have been crushed. My marriage with my husband, Wayne, was a good marriage. We had faced various trials in our lives together. We clung to each other and to God during those times. We also enjoyed many joyful moments together. Wayne was a loving husband and we enjoyed children, new daughters-in-law, and grandchildren together. Our dream was for a happy retirement together. That dream was shattered by his diagnosis in 2006. His neurological disease led to his continual deterioration physically and his eventual death in early 2011.

Family care-giving brings on a storm of problems and emotions. It creates havoc and sometimes destroys one's former way of life. Yet even in the storms, even when our dreams are smashed into a million pieces, God is still with us. His promises from His Word are still true. When we are in God's powerful hands, there is no safer place to be in spite of the care-giving storms that may be raging around us.

God also has a new and good life planned for both the caregiver and his or her loved one. For my husband, Wayne, that was a life in Heaven with Jesus. For me, although I grieve my husband's absence from me, it is other ministry for the Lord. For other caregivers, it may be the earthly healing of the loved one and wonderful ministries for both of them in God's service. God wants us to leave the outcomes of our lives in His hands, to rest in peace in Him, and to keep our eyes focused on Him and not on our problems. He will help us weather the waves of life's storms. Sometimes it is hard to understand why we have to face the difficult storms of life. Yet trusting in the Lord and in His promises will give us more peace than knowing all the answers to our questions.

Dear caregiver, even in the midst of your care-giving storms the Lord is providing for you. He is able to do wonders for you even while the storm is raging. He cares about and provides for the big problems and the relatively insignificant problems. Trust Him and obey Him in the process. God's provision for you will never run out. Your trust in God and faithfulness to God while in the storm will also be noticed by others and, in turn, bring glory to God.

In the midst of this care-giving storm you have two choices, dear caregiver. You can stress and wring your hands in anxiety, or you can trust God's faithfulness and power to see you through it. Make the choice to meditate on God's promises and praise Him. Don't focus on the problems, but focus on the Lord. One way or another, the storm will quiet in God's perfect timing.

The Tightrope of Care-giving

On June 15, 2012, some of you may have seen televised Nik Wallenda's dream come true as he walked across Niagara Falls between the U.S. and Canada on a tightrope. He covered the 1,800 feet in approximately 25 minutes, walking the two-inch wire in elk skin-soled shoes and using a balance beam. Now, I would not recommend viewing Niagara Falls in this fashion. One might even argue the wisdom and even rightness of taking such a risk. I think there are lessons we can learn from this incident, however.

Much of life — and certainly care-giving — is filled with challenges. Because of the uncertainties and constant changes and declines of care-giving, it can feel as if one is in imminent danger. During care-giving days, one is not able to predict what the next year, let alone the next month or day will bring. It can feel like one is walking in a fog on a tightrope. As Wallenda made his walk across Niagara Falls, he found the heavy mist to be very challenging. Also, the winds hit him and were definitely more than he expected. After a period of time, his forearms started to tense up and he began experiencing numbness. The steps and days as a caregiver can feel the same way.

ABC televised the walk, but insisted Wallenda use a safety tether to prevent him from plunging into the roaring waters of Niagara Falls should he fall. I do not know how great a safety measure this was in reality, but I do know that Christian caregivers have a wonderful source of strength and safety in the Lord Jesus Christ. Care-giving can feel like walking over stormy waters, but the Lord is a reliable source of safety. Also, Wallenda walked across that tightrope putting one foot in front of the other. That is what Christian caregivers and all believers need to do. They need to take life one step at a time, focusing on the Lord and trusting Him.

When Wallenda stepped onto Canadian soil, he was immediately asked for his passport, which he extracted from a protective pouch in his jacket. To me, that passport is a picture of God's Word and its promises. It is what helps us walk the tightrope and stormy situations of life, like care-giving.

Wallenda said that the prayers of others helped him immensely. He said it helped him reach the safety of the other side. So we too need to be willing to ask for and rely on the prayers of others when we are going through stormy times. Wallenda further said that in the middle of the wire he started thinking about his great-grandfather. His family's legacy for performing daredevil stunts is what helped him persevere to the end. So we also can follow the examples of the Biblical saints and our godly ancestors who have gone before us. Their past faith can encourage us to be faithful and to trust God.

Christian caregiver, walk step by step, focusing on the Lord as you experience the stormy waters of caregiving. Rely on God's Word and prayer. Trust that God will get you to the other side.

Joy

Care-giving for a family member with a terminal illness is one of life's most difficult experiences. It is stressful and very discouraging at times. This is especially true if a caregiver is forced to helplessly watch his or her loved one continue to deteriorate in health step by step. I know this is true because I was my husband's caregiver for four and a half years.

Remember, however, that joy is possible in even these circumstances. This is because joy and difficulty — and even joy and sorrow — can coexist. Joy is also possible in the challenges and heartaches of care-giving because joy is not dependent on circumstances. True joy is experienced as a result of living in the presence of the Lord and through deep communication with Him.

True joy and peace is experienced when we know God is with us in those difficult situations; it is knowing that He is keeping us, protecting us, and strengthening us in those situations. Joy and peace is knowing the Lord God is in control. Someone sent me this formula for joy and strength: Thankfulness = joy = strength. If we can somehow thank God in all things, knowing and trusting that He is indeed in control and loves us deeply, we can began to experience joy. Joy then turns into strength to face life's challenges (Nehemiah 8:10b).

Spend time in God's Word, dear caregiver. Revel in and latch on to His promises in His Word. Spend time in prayer. Ask for His strength and joy. Care-giving can be so overwhelmingly difficult and emotionally challenging. However, even in those very difficult days, dear caregiver, you can find joy in the Lord. He will get you through those days step by step. Though you do not know what lies ahead, He will lead you. He will give you His strength and joy.

The four and a half years of my husband's illness and the years since his death have included greater dependence on the Lord's strength, God revealing His grace in awesome ways, and God leading me step by step when I didn't know what I was doing (Psalm 32:8). These years have further included a closer and more precious relationship with the Lord than ever before, God's faithfulness shown to me, returning and new joy in the Lord in spite of waves of grief (which, though smaller, still hit), greater empathy for others, and new areas of service. Finally, these years have included the Lord being my heavenly bridegroom (Isaiah 54:5). I've learned to depend upon His Word. Ecclesiastes 3 tells us that there is a time for everything and everything is beautiful in its time. It has not always felt that way, but through it all the Lord has been with me. He will be with you also, dear Christian caregiver. Rest in the joy of the Lord. That is your strength, dear Christian caregiver.

Him in You,
Interceding for You

*F*amily care-giving is one of life's most difficult and challenging experiences. I know this to be a fact, because I was a family caregiver. Yet the Bible tells us to actually delight in difficulties (II Corinthians 12:10). When I was a caregiver, I was thankful if I could just survive and have strength for the day. Why would anyone welcome trials and difficulties in their lives? Well, for one thing, it gives us an opportunity to trust the Lord. It also gives us an opportunity to experience His sufficient grace and strength in us (II Corinthians 12:9).

Family care-giving is often discouraging and physically and emotionally draining. It can often bring on feelings of hopelessness and despair. In spite of this, dear Christian caregiver, you have the same power in you as it took to raise Jesus Christ from the dead. You have resurrection power in you, dear caregiver! (Ephesians 1:18-20.) Don't concentrate on your own puny, insufficient strength. Concentrate on the Lord's mighty strength in you, dear caregiver!

After Jesus arose from the dead, He was seated in the heavenly realms at the Father's right hand. He has all authority and power at His disposal (Ephesians 1:20b-23). He delights in placing that same power that belongs to Him in you, dear caregiver! Also, His love for you is deeper and wider and higher than you can begin to imagine! (Ephesians 3:16-19.)

Finally, as Jesus the Son of God is sitting next to the Father; He is interceding for you, dear Christian caregiver. The Son of God actually lives to intercede for you and for all His people! (Hebrews 7:25b.) He knows how weak and tired you often feel in the whole care-giving scenario, so He gives you His power and love and intercedes for you to the Father. Picture the Son sitting next to the Father, talking with Him about your needs and the needs of your loved one! Isn't that an awesome thought, dear caregiver? Revel in that thought and rest in Him!

Wait on the Lord

About a year after my husband was diagnosed with his disease, I was diagnosed with breast cancer. Here are some of the thoughts and prayers that were running through my mind after my diagnosis of breast cancer on July 18, 2007:

I don't understand, Lord. You have been faithful to me in numerous times of difficulty in the past. This latest trial in my life seems a bit overwhelming, however, Lord. Was not dealing with the emotional stress of my husband's disabling neurological disease enough, Lord? Did I have to receive a diagnosis of breast cancer also?

Of one thing I was certain, however. Even though I did not always understand His ways, I knew my Lord did not make mistakes. I could count on His promises in His Holy Word, His eternal love for me, and His infinite wisdom. I could count on these things even when feeling emotionally downcast. I could count on the fact that God's compassion for me would never fail. He, in His faithfulness, would have new blessings for me every day. One other thing of which I was certain was that I had nothing or no one else I could cling to but the Lord. He alone was able to be my hope. I needed to wait on the Lord to work out His plan in my life. (Lamentations 3:20b-26.) I also believed that somehow God would make a place of refreshment and joy out of the deep valleys of my life. He was indeed the only One, but He was the capable One to help me proceed in His strength in facing life's huge hurdles (Psalm 84:6-7).

We have the certainty of the Lord's faithfulness and love even in the harshest of circumstances. In the Old Testament book of Lamentations, the author was lamenting or mourning the destruction of Jerusalem and the temple. Hence, he was feeling very discouraged and depressed. Have you ever felt like the author of Lamentations? When we begin to feel like the author of Lamentations felt, we are beginning to focus on ourselves instead of on the Lord. The truth of the matter is that there is always the certainty of the Lord's presence, even in the worst of circumstances. It is not necessary for our circumstances to change to experience the Lord's joy and peace in our hearts and lives. We just need to take our focus off of ourselves and our problems and focus on the Lord.

When we are feeling discouraged by a difficult set of circumstances in our lives, we must remember the Lord's love for us and the Lord's awesome promises in His Holy Word. The Lord's river of mercy and love never runs dry. People, material possessions and our own resources will often fail us. The Lord, however, will never fail us! His love and faithfulness is with us moment by moment and day by day. How precious it is to awaken each morning knowing that the Lord will be walking beside us each day as we face daily stresses and challenges. Wait on the Lord, dear caregiver. Waiting on the Lord means we are resting our entire trust in the Lord for time and eternity. We can trust completely in the Lord's unfailing love! Praise His name!

Lessons We Need to Learn

When we are stripped of the things we are depending on outside of the Lord and when we are stripped of thinking we are strong in ourselves, we begin to trust and lean on the Lord instead. We begin to see how weak we really are without the Lord. In this place of desperate clinging to the Lord, our acknowledgment of our weakness makes room for the power of God in our lives. It also makes our love for God become more intense. Care-giving — with all of its overwhelming challenges — and the years since my husband's death have taught me the lesson of how weak I am in myself and how desperately I need the Lord. It may have done the same for you, dear caregiver. That is actually a good place to be, for here you reach out for God's all powerful strength.

Fear and love for the Lord do not belong together, because love that flows from God and is perfected by God drives out and removes fears (I John 4:18). So often during my care-giving days for my husband I succumbed to fear about the future and sometimes even fear of what that day would bring. Yet the Lord commands us over and over in Scripture to not be afraid.

The Lord also holds us when we are overwhelmed by life's trials. He holds us and comforts us and loves us during those times. The Lord knows your care-giving sorrows, dear caregiver, and He loves and comforts you through the process. You know He loves you because He sacrificed His very life for you on the cross. He has proven His love for you, dear care-giver!

In Scripture, the devil is portrayed as a roaring lion who wants to devour us. The devil knows when we are at our lowest and weakest and loves to try to prey on us in those moments. God's advice is to humble ourselves before God and not be anxious, because He cares for us and will protect us. His advice is to also stand firm in our

faith (I Peter 5:6-9). It is so easy in the care-giving scenario to become discouraged. Yet the Lord has promised
to be with us, if we turn to Him.

Dear caregiver, trust in the Lord's strength, not your
own. When you recognize your own weakness and lean
on the Lord's strength, you are strong. Do not fear, for
the Lord is with you. Rest in His love. Also avail yourself of His comforting arms around you. Finally, be alert
for the devil's attempts to discourage you. Turn to the
Lord instead.

The Potter

The Bible teaches us that the Lord God is the Potter in our lives, and we are the clay in His hands. He is in sovereign control of our lives, and He controls all the events of our lives. All the events of our lives are used to make us more like Jesus. God especially uses problems, difficulties, and trials in our lives to mold us into the kind of people who truly reflect the Lord Jesus. The Lord wants to bring us ever closer to the center of His will. This is also true about the difficult challenges and trials of family care-giving. Difficulties teach us not to rely on our own efforts and devices. Difficult times in our lives teach us to rely and trust only on the Lord. This became abundantly clear to me when I was a caregiver for my husband. His disease was incurable. It was out of my control. The only recourse was to seek to rely on and trust in the Lord.

Difficulties in our lives also help to remove the impurities of sin from our lives, and they help us to grow in our love relationship with the Lord. When spiritual impurities come into our lives, the Lord God recreates and molds our lives to be more in tune with His will. Our prayer to God should be that He will make us into beautiful vessels of purpose for Him. When we fail and allow spiritual impurities into our lives, we need to pray that the Lord will take us back to His Potter's wheel. We need to pray that the Lord will then reshape us and form us into something more beautiful for Him. From the broken fragments of our lives, the Lord can make us into beautiful vessels for Him!

From experience, I know the pressure of family caregiving can feel overwhelming and unbearable at times. We must not fight against or question the Lord's molding of our lives, however. We need to pray that each touch of the Lord's hand on our lives will help us to become who He wants us to become. The Lord knows just the right amount of pressure to put on our lives. We must also remain thankful for how He has made us and thankful for how He is working and leading in our lives! We must persevere in our willingness to submit to the Lord's will. We must be submissive to the Lord even in trials and difficult times in our lives. The Lord has promised to be with us all the way.

Finally, we must also ask the Lord for the filling of the Holy Spirit's power and the fruit of the Holy Spirit in our lives. We must yearn for the Lord to control our lives completely every hour and every day! Dear caregiver, trust your life and your care-giving journey to the hand of the great Potter. He knows what He is doing even when the path becomes very difficult.

Caregiver Worries

There are many stresses and challenges which accompany being a family caregiver. This is especially true for the caregiver who is caring for a loved one who has a long-standing terminal illness. It is easy for the caregiver to fall into the pit of fear and discouragement. There are often fears and worries about just getting through the day and also for the future. I remember experiencing these stresses and fears as a caregiver for my husband.

The Lord God wants us to release those worries to Him. This is so very difficult to do when the challenges are so overwhelming. In the measure we release those worries to the Lord and seek Him, the more we will experience His peace, however.

The Lord God loves you with an everlasting love, dear Christian caregiver. Our minds are not able to fully comprehend His unfailing love. Our emotions often fluctuate and falter in the face of difficult circumstances. I know this was true of me as a caregiver and is also true of me since my care-giving days. God's love and faithfulness always remain constant, however. Cling to that, dear Christian caregiver.

Remember too, dear caregiver, that God is sovereign over your life and the life of the loved one for whom you are caring. He is in control. Caregivers have to manage so many things for their loved ones. They not only have to care for their love one's needs, but they also often have to be their loved one's advocate. As a caregiver, I sometimes felt as if I was the only one who cared about my husband's well-being. Perhaps you feel the same way, dear caregiver. This can be a lonely feeling.

Know, however, that God is in control. Trust Him for your future and your loved one's future. Also, thank Him each day for blessings that are still in your life. Trust and thankfulness are the keys to peace. Is not that a better alternative to worry and wringing of the hands that does absolutely no good?

Trust the Lord, dear caregiver. Give Him your worries and concerns for your loved one. He is in control and He will be faithful to you all the way.

Him Bearing Your Burdens

*T*he path of being a caregiver for a family member is sometimes so steep and so exhausting. If caregivers carry a load of fear and sometimes false guilt on their backs, the way is going to be even more difficult. If a loved one is terminally ill and deteriorating month by month before a caregiver's eyes, it is so easy for fear of the future to set in. It is also easy to feel a sense of false guilt when a caregiver witnesses these things in his or her love one's life. As a caregiver, I remember having these feelings. The truth of the matter is that it is totally irrational to fear or feel guilty about the uncontrollable.

It is important at such times to remember that God is the one who is in control of our lives and not us. The Lord God also wants to remove the heavy emotional loads we put on ourselves. In Matthew 11:28-30 in the Bible, the Lord invites us to come to Him when we feel weary and emotionally weighed down, and He promises to give His rest. He invites us to yoke or tie our lives to Him, and He promises to lighten our load. He will then be carrying our load. This is the way to true freedom.

It is His unconditional love and presence that can free you, dear caregiver, from fears and negative emotions. Spend time in His presence each day through prayer and Bible reading. Bask in the light of His promises and presence in this way. Your care-giving heartaches and problems will not magically go away, but the Lord will be beside you each step of the way.

The Tapestry of our Lives

*R*omans 8:28 in the Bible promises us that in both the pleasant circumstances and in the tragic circumstances of life, God is working for our good. This promise is a blessed promise. We can rest in that promise and trust in it when the world around us seems to be falling apart, but it is also a promise with which we may at times struggle.

I remember first struggling with the promise of Romans 8:28 when my dad was suffering the excruciating pain of cancer and radiation. I wondered how "all things" could possibly be working for good in this case? It is also something I pondered when my husband was diagnosed with a devastating neurological disease. It was something I thought about when I was struggling with the challenges of care-giving, and I saw the effects my husband's disease was having on his body. It was something I was confused about when my husband passed away four and a half years later.

The key to understanding this verse is to realize that not all things are good in themselves. Sin has wreaked havoc with our world, and there are many experiences in this world that are not good or pleasant in themselves. God, however, works both the "good" and the "bad" events of our lives together for our ultimate good.

It has been said that life is like a tapestry. When you look at the backside of a tapestry, it does not look beautiful. There are knotted-off ends and threads that seem to have no meaning or beauty. When one turns the tapestry over, however, one sees a beautiful picture or design.

Dear caregiver, when you see the difficulties and heartaches of care-giving, you are seeing only the backside of the tapestry of life. God, however, is bringing all the threads or events of our lives together — both the good and bad — into a beautiful tapestry. The Lord already sees the top part of our tapestry of life. The Lord already sees the beautiful end result of what He is accomplishing in our lives. When we do not understand the reason for the difficult circumstances in our lives and in the lives of our loved ones, we must simply trust that the Lord is working out all things in our lives for His glory and to accomplish His plan. He is also working out all things for our ultimate spiritual good.

The ultimate spiritual good that the Lord God is seeking to accomplish in our lives is that we might become more like Jesus every day in our thoughts, attitudes, and actions (Romans 8:29). In order for this to happen, there must be a conforming process taking place in our lives. This conforming process often can only occur during times of trial and difficulty in our lives. Gelatin is only able to be conformed or shaped to the mold into which it is placed after it has been dissolved in hot water. So we often have to go through the heat of trials and difficulties to become more conformed to the likeness of Jesus.

God has the pattern for our lives all figured out. He knows and understands the beautiful tapestry that He is weaving for our lives. He knows the beginning from the end. We must trust the Lord to do His beautiful work in our lives, even in times when life's events and circumstances seem very difficult and overwhelming!

Never Separated from Christ's Love

Sometimes the future can seem so uncertain and fearful to a caregiver of a loved one with a terminal illness. As a caregiver, I remember having such fears. As children of God, however, we have victory in Christ Jesus our Lord! We need to fear nothing, for the Lord is on our side! Nothing can separate us from the love of God! What an awesome thought, and what an awesome promise! In light of all this, there can be overflowing joy in our hearts!

We are secure in Christ for time and for eternity. Sometimes we may feel as if everything is against us, but the Word of God teaches us that the great God of the universe is always for us and is always with us! (Romans

8:31-32.) God proved His love for us by sending His only Son to die for our sins. Surely we can trust Him to provide us with everything we need for time and eternity. In the uncertainties of life, Christian caregivers can rest in the Lord. They have the Lord God on their side, and they are victors in Him!

Nothing will happen to us that are not in God's plan for our lives, so we need not fear. Finally, Christ is always interceding for His children before God the Father! He is interceding for you, dear Christian caregiver! He knows your heartaches, your challenges, and your fears; and He is praying for you! What a blessed promise!

In light of all this, what set of circumstances can ever separate you from the love of Christ, dear Christian caregiver? (Romans 8:35.) The answer is that nothing can separate us from the love of Christ! No matter what hardships, trials, or heartaches you may be experiencing in your life at the moment, you are never separated from the love of Christ.

What is more, Romans 8:37 teaches you that you are more than a conqueror! You become a conqueror through the trials of care-giving by patiently enduring these trials and by being submissive to the Lord's will. You become more than a conqueror by using these experiences to grow in your love and service for the Lord.

God always see us through difficult times and brings us to ultimate victory. He will do the same for you, dear Christian caregiver. Victory is always assured for the Christian — if not in this life, then in eternity. Your loved one may be healed on this earth, or he or she may be healed in eternity. There will be victory for your loved one either way. There will be victory for you too, dear caregiver. If your loved one goes to live with the Lord, you may feel as if your life has been shattered in a million pieces; but God will bring ultimate victory and peace for you also.

Absolutely nothing will ever separate us from the love of God and the victory we have in the Lord Jesus Christ! (Romans 8:38-39.) Praise the name of the Lord for our victory in Him!

The Caregiver's
Rest and Peace

*F*amily caregivers often face huge obstacles. Although care-giving for a loved one is an extremely important mission in life, it is also often physically and emotionally exhausting. Caregivers must find their rest, confidence, help, and peace in the Lord alone. Psalm 62 in the Old Testament of the Bible says that God alone must be our rock or firm foundation and our fortress or source of protection.

Family caregivers — and all of us, for that matter — can and must find our confidence and help in the Lord alone. If we put our confidence in anything or anyone but the Lord, we will often be disappointed. However, we can go to the Lord at any moment and any place and He will be our help and strength.

Hence, the Lord alone is the caregiver's source of peace and repose in the heartaches and discouraging events of care-giving. As a caregiver, watching my husband's body deteriorate often made me feel very discouraged. Psalm 62 reminds the caregiver — and all of us — that no matter what we are facing we need never be shaken, because the Lord is our rock or foundation. He is our sure foundation, even when it seems as if our world is crumbling and falling down around us. The Lord is also our salvation. He is our Savior from our sins. He further saves us from many unseen perils and pitfalls each and every day. The Lord is our fortress or protection. Hence, no matter what is going on in our lives, we need never give up and be anxious in our spirits.

Family caregiving can present many difficult challenges. In spite of all life's troubles, however, we all must learn the secret of waiting and resting in the Lord. So often, when we face a crisis in our lives we try to work out the adverse situation or circumstances by our own devices. Often, we go to the Lord only as a last resort.

We need to go to the Lord first. Rest and peace for our souls can be found in the Lord God alone. Then nothing can ultimately shake us. No matter what the situation, we can trust the Lord and rest in Him in quiet submission. Our well-being for time and for eternity depends on the Lord God alone. He is our sure foundation and refuge.

We have the absolute assurance of the Lord's protecting presence in our lives at all times. Thus, Psalm 62 reminds us to trust in God in all situations and at all times. We must pour out our hearts to Him for help in facing the difficult situations, for God is our help and refuge. The Lord will never fail us. The Lord understands us and our needs perfectly. The Lord understands our needs and sympathizes with us better than anyone else is able to do. Resorting to our own devices to get us through a crisis will prove to be of no avail, but our God is our refuge and help. We serve a faithful God. We also serve a loving and powerful God! If we trust in the Lord, He will direct our paths! He will direct your path also, dear Christian caregiver! You can count on it!

Rock of Security

There are many things going on in this world which could cause us to succumb to fear. Watching one's loved one's health continue to deteriorate step by step is a time in life when it is so easy to fall prey to fear. Isaiah 51 in the Old Testament of the Bible offers comfort when we feel we are becoming entangled in the tentacles of fear. Take time to read the first few verses of this chapter in the Bible, dear caregiver. A child of God need not and must not be controlled by fear. When we begin to fear anything, we must quickly run to the Lord for comfort and protection. The Lord in His sovereignty already has our lives all planned, so we need not fear.

When we begin to sink into despair or fear for any reason, the Lord desires that we listen to Him and seek Him. He is the rock of security which we can always

307

count on (Isaiah 51:1). We who are the Lord's children and are seeking to live for Him can look to Jesus, our rock and foundation. Jesus is the rock which we need to turn to in times of great fear. The Lord Jesus gives our lives a sure foundation, even in times of uncertainty and fear.

Verse two of Isaiah 51 also suggests that we can follow the examples of the Biblical heroes of faith for inspiration in our own walk of faith. Hebrews 11 in the New Testament of the Bible gives a wonderful account of many of these Biblical heroes of faith. Furthermore, we can emulate the examples of people in our current life who are walking in faith without fear and with a sure confidence in their Lord. These people are all links in the chain of faith, and they can be an inspiration to us.

Isaiah 51:3a promised God's Old Testament people that God would comfort them and would look with compassion on all their heartaches. The Lord promised He would turn the deserts of their lives into something beautiful. The Lord will comfort you also, dear Christian caregiver, when you go through fearful or difficult situations as you care for your loved one. Somehow, in His power and grace, He will turn the deserts of your life into blessings. As a believer in the Lord Jesus Christ, you will proceed from victory to victory. No ultimate spiritual harm can ever come to a child of God. Even if you or your love one dies, you will immediately go to be with the Lord. What have we to fear? Among God's people there need not be crippling fear, but rather joy, thanksgiving, and singing! (Isaiah 51:3b.)

You need fear nothing, dear caregiver, because our faithful God is always with you to comfort and protect you and your loved one (Isaiah 51:12a). With the Lord on your side, you need never retreat or cower in fear. The Lord can diffuse any situation, even difficult and overwhelming care-giving situations! The great Lord of the universe personally cares about and loves you! He knows you by name, dear Christian caregiver. He knows everything about you. He has you and your loved one's entire future planned out moment by moment! You may not always understand His ways and why He allows certain things in your life, but you can trust that He is in control and loves you. He will always give comfort and strength enough for every difficult and fearful situation in our lives! Rest your life in Him in joy and thanksgiving!

Do Not Live in Fear

$C$are-giving and watching my husband decline in his health, and then his death in January of 2011 has been one of my life's most difficult tests. Knowing I could trust that God loved me and was in control in the midst of the confusion and grief of it all made, and continues to make, all the difference in the world.

God is sovereign and in control. Nothing happens to a Christian caregiver or his or her loved one that is not filtered through His love. This is true even in the heartbreaking events which often accompany care-giving, and sometimes the loved one's death. This is a difficult truth to accept. When this truth is accepted, however, it a soft place to land when one is overwhelmed with life's difficulties.

God is good. Circumstances may be bad, but God is good. God is the very definition and essence of goodness.

He proved that by sending His Son on the cross. He can help caregivers who are struggling to keep emotional and spiritual equilibrium in the midst of the heartaches of seeing their loved ones decline in their health. He can also slowly heal caregivers emotionally when and if their loved ones are not healed on this earth.

Joy can coexist in the midst of the heartaches and grief that often accompany care-giving and possibly losing our loved ones. This is because joy is not based on circumstances which are favorable or perfect. Rather, it is based on a relationship with the Lord. If the Lord takes your loved one to Himself sooner than you would like, dear caregiver, He will be with you each step of the way then also. There is deep hurt and grief in the loss of a love one. It involves a process that takes much time and deep crying out to the Lord and depending on Him. There is a scar that never goes completely away. Yet, the Lord's faithfulness will be with you all the way, and the joy of the Lord will return. Do not live in fear of the future, dear Christian caregiver. Never forget that the Lord loves you, and He is good. He is in control.

CPSIA information can be obtained at www.ICGtesting.com
Printed in the USA
LVOW01s2111170414

382159LV00002B/2/P